Pioneer Potpourri

Rosalind Batterbee Bundy Westcott

~✦~

Compiled by
Dawn Batterbee Miller
DawnCreations.net

DP

Quality Publishing Services

Pioneer Potpourri
by Rosalind Batterbee Bundy Westcott

Published by DocUmeant Publishing
14 Wall St 20th Floor
NY, NY 10005
www.DocUmeantPublishing.com

646-233-4366

Front Cover Design: Dawn Batterbee Miller
www.DawnCreations.net

Back Cover Design: Ginger Marks,
www.DocUmeantDesigns.com

Design & Layout: Ginger Marks

Compiled and edited by: Dawn Batterbee Miller

LOCC-style: F572.64W471995

Published in The United States
First publishing date: 01/1995
Second edition: 08/2007

ISBN 13: 978-0-9788831-3-3 12.50
ISBN 10: 0978883136

CONTENTS

iv

Introduction

With the compilation of Pioneer Potpourri Rosalind Batterbee Bundy Westcott, at age 85, sees her dream of publishing a book of her writings fulfilled. This is done with the assistance of her niece, Dawn Batterbee Miller, herself a published author.

The article and photo following appear here to allow the reader to experience with them the joy of accomplishment that can be attained even at a time when others may think it not possible.

Our hope is that it may inspire you to reach for your dream no matter the obstacles in your mind.

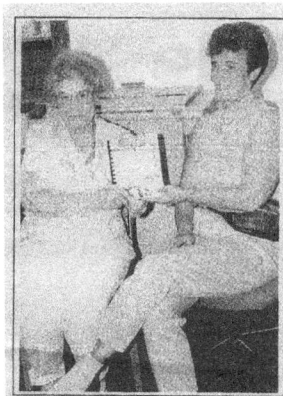

HOLDING A COPY of Rosalind Wescott's first book are Rosalind (left) and her niece Dawn Miller, who is working on a historical novel set in the Antrim-Charlevoix county area.

Local author plans book signing

She was born in 1910, the first of 11 children born to Harry E. Batterbee and Celestia Warden.

Now Rosalind Batterbee Bundy Westcott has published a book featuring collected tales and personal remembrances of those long-ago days of the early settlement of Antrim and Charlevoix counties.

"The book was really not my idea. But my oldest brother's daughter, Dawn Miller, thought (the material) ought to be kept," said the East Jordan resident in a recent interview.

Westcott says she always had a flair for writing. By age 10, she was writing fantasy stories about an ice princess.

As she grew up, Westcott continued writing children's stories. Later the stories made regular appearances in Mancelona, Bellaire and other area newspapers.

Sometime after that Westcott began a column called "Looking Around Jordan Township" that appeared in local newspapers for years.

In addition to her own observations about life and nature, Westcott wrote about the history of other families in the area, or allowed others to tell their stories through her column. Prodded by Miller, Westcott began going through the old columns last fall.

Westcott's first book, *Pioneer Potpourri*, was published this year. Those interested in the book or in meeting the author might want to circle two dates in their calendars:

■ On Sat., Sept. 16, from 11 a.m. to 1 p.m. there will be a book signing at Busy Bridge Antiques and Gifts, 207 Main, East Jordan.

■ On Thurs., Sept. 21, from 7-9 p.m. there will be a book signing at the Mancelona Public Library at 202 W. State Street.

Forward

The project began one spring day in 1994 when my husband and I drove north to East Jordan, Michigan for a visit with 83 year old Aunt Rosie. Two years earlier she had been diagnosed with cancer, but she had surprised everybody. Instead of giving up and dying, she had regained her strength and had left the hospital.

"I was ready for God to take me home," she declared, "but as long as I'm here I'll do all I can for him." She resumed teaching Sunday School, held Bible studies in her home and counseled people in her community.

In her day, Aunt Rosie had written a column for weekly newspapers, and she loved to reminisce about her career. During that visit I asked her to tell me how she had started writing professionally. "I was in my forties then," she said. "Sometimes I'd see an interesting house and I'd stop by and talk to whoever was there. They all had stories to tell."

"I'd love to read your columns," I told her.

"Just a minute," she said. Then she began to rummage through a drawer, and soon she pulled out a brown-covered scrapbook and handed it to me.

Pasted inside were scores of articles, many about the pioneers of northern Michigan which she called the wild, wild Midwest. Thumbing through the brittle pages, I read about Sam Wildfong, who had crossed a Great Lakes passage in a rowboat with his family of five. There was a story about William Stevens, a Pony Express rider who had been shot in the hip and crippled during a battle with Indians. I saw an account about the Kocher children, who had to keep a sharp lookout on their way to school, "as and occasional bear was seen."

I closed the scrapbook and handed it back to her. "Aunt Rosie, this is beautiful."

Take it with you," she urged. "I'd be glad for you to look at it."

At home the next day I settled back with a cup of coffee and began to read. Immediately, I was swept up in Aunt Rosie's stories. The more I read, the more I began to think that her writing ought to be preserved in something better than an old scrapbook. Perhaps even in a book.

Why not? I thought. I had a photo copier and a plastic spiral binder I could use. *Aunt Rosie will be so pleased!*

I took the scrapbook apart, page by page and photocopied the articles. After several days, Aunt Rosie's writings covered the sofa and the coffee table and everything in the room.

I typed a table of contents and prepared an author's page, cutting a hole in the paper and pasting Aunt Rosie's photograph behind it. I added a biographical sketch and a copy of her press card.

When I went back to East Jordan and showed her the project, Aunt Rosie was thrilled. "I've always dreamed of writing a book," she said.

What shall I name it? I asked.

She only hesitated for a moment.

"Pioneer Potpourri," she declared, her eyes sparkling.

I put together six copies—enough for Aunt Rosie, me and a few other family members. The print was uneven, some pages dark and some light, and the columns of type didn't always line up. But after working on the project for three weeks I was glad to be finished.

"Dawn, this is great!" my brother Cliff exclaimed as he thumbed through the pages. "Everyone in the family is going to want one." He took a five dollar bill out of his wallet. "This should get you started. I'm paying for mine."

I was flabbergasted. I had just wanted to make Aunt Rosie happy. Besides, I couldn't sell a book that looked like this. I'd have to retype the whole thing and clean up the format. This is more than I bargained for.

"We'll work together," Aunt Rosie said the next time I visited. "We'll organize the articles in chronological order, and I'll give each one a new title. I can rewrite the columns that were lost." I hadn't seen her that excited in a long time.

I went home and resumed typing with renewed determination. I thought of Aunt Rosie and her eyes glowing as we worked together. How pleased she was at the prospect of finally publishing a book.

Then I came upon half dozen articles about my own family. I learned about the kidnapping of my great-uncle Jasper. And about my great-great-grandpa Warden's adventures during the Civil War. And then about my grandpa Batterbee moving to the old logging camp that became our family home. The more I learned the more interested I became.

Each morning I hurried through my chores to get back to Aunt Rosie's book. By spring the finished manuscript ran to 118 pages. Thousands of photocopies cluttered the house as my husband and I began the process of collating, punching holes and stringing plastic coils through the holes. Finally the project was complete—36 beautiful books.

At our family reunion outside of Lansing in July, we put copies of *Pioneer Potpourri* on a table. Aunt Rosie sat there, smiling proudly as she autographed them for relatives. By the end of the day only four copies were left.

"Could you make a few more?" Aunt Rosie asked. "I could sell them to my friends."

"Sure," I replied. So I made 100 more copies.

Then I had another idea, "Why don't we have a book signing?" She agreed, so I made arrangements with a library and an antique store. I called a reporter and two weeks later an announcement ran in the local newspaper, complete with Aunt Rosie's picture.

In August, Aunt Rosie entered the hospital for knee surgery. "Get me over this quickly," she told the doctor. "I have a book signing in two weeks!"

But the surgery was too much for Aunt Rosie. Two days after the operation she went to be with the Lord. I was left to handle the signings on my own.

"Don't' feel bad," her daughter Ardith told me. "Mother died looking forward to something special. Her life was productive to the end."

I have sold several hundred copies of Aunt Rosie's books, in states from Michigan to Florida. They are in libraries, schools and historical archives. The project has become one of the most satisfying things I have ever done. What started out as a good deed for an elderly aunt became a mission for me.

The preceding is an article published in Guideposts in June of 1998. After the story was published, sales increased 100 fold. The book has sold across the U.S.A. from Michigan to Florida— from New York to California. People went to great lengths to contact me and buy a book. It is available in the Library of Michigan and has even been used as daily reading on a radio program in New York State.

I hope you enjoy my Aunt Rosie's publication.

Dawn Batterbee Miller

SECTION 1
Early Pioneers

Northland

One March morning the flowers that lay beneath the leaves and the little seeds that had fallen the year before woke suddenly and decided they had slept long enough. "It is time to awake," they said. "We must get out into the sunshine."

"But," said one timid violet, "what if we woke too early? Let's send some hardy one ahead to see if winter is really gone."

"I'll second that," spoke up Beth Lily. "We will wait." So they sent Spring Beauty, which pleased Beauty very much. He liked being the first flower of spring, for he knew he received special attention because of it.

So Spring Beauty stretched his arms above his head and pushed his toes deeper into the earth. Up on his toes he stood, stretching and stretching until at last his tiny hands went right through the surface; at once he felt the warm sun. Throwing wide his arms he pushed up and up until he reached his full height. Then, turning quickly to face the sun and opening his eyes, he looked around.

Yes, there was Miss May Flower, hiding beneath her own leaves as usual, just waiting to be called. May liked to be up early too, but she just couldn't wake until someone called her.

May is a hardy girl though, a true northerner who doesn't go below the ground to spend the winter but pulls her own leaves over her head and goes to sleep while winter winds blow. Then at first call she stretches her limbs and wakes in a moment. So May Flower is always second to arrive in the spring.

A warm breeze fanned the cheek of Spring Beauty, turning the leaves and melting the last bits of snow they hid. "Wake up, everyone," Spring Beauty called. "Wake up. Spring is come!!!"

At once May Flowers stretched their heads above their leafy covers to smile at the world, and the green tips of Adders Tongue and Beth Lilies began to appear. Buds swelled upon the trees and tiny new leaves peeped out. The impatient Wild Plum did not wait for leaves to form but burst immediately into a beautiful cloud of bloom.

As the last banks of snow on the slopes melted and ran down into the valleys, soaking the roots of plants and trees in the pastures and woodlands, the west wind whispered softly over the earth and the old autumn leaves that lay in repose rustled in their beds.

The brook that chattered and gurgled so pleasantly in summer, took on a new and deeper tone as it rushed along, carrying away the debris of winter and taking great bites of soil from the edges of its banks. Rumbling and roaring along, it gained more speed and power as it neared the valley. To any one listening it seemed to be warning the world to keep out of its way.

As the flowers grew, each one bringing forth its own beautiful blossoms, the woods and fields took on a new life and beauty.

But the flowers were not alone, for many of nature's children came scampering from their dens, and high overhead their feathered friends and enemies fluttered and flew.

Yes, spring had returned to the Northland, each segment in its own way. And all things welcomed the SPRING

INTROSPECTION

Autumn is here, yes autumn is here,
Autumn was my favorite time of the year.
I'd romp in the wind and shriek with the cold,
Never dreaming that one day I would be old —
That my limbs would be stiff,
And my back would be sore;
So I never could run with the wind any more.

Now when autumn comes, it's a whole different story.
I still love the season; in its colors I glory.
I watch the children as like leaves they scatter,
While I sit in the sun—but my age doesn't matter;
For once I was young, tho' it doesn't seem real.
I understand and I know how they feel.

One day autumn will be here again;
The children, the colors, the wind and the rain.
They all will arrive, each in its own season,
Romping and shrieking without rhyme or reason.
Though I will not hear them, it still is my pleasure
To dream of the old days and the mem'ries I treasure.

THE GRAPEVINE

They tell me there is a great city which sits on a hill,
And it's called the Holy Jerusalem.

They say too, that one day I may see it; that I may pass a
wall of jasper, thu' gates of pearl;
And walk on streets of gold that appear as clear as glass.
> I, whose feet have more often trod bare floors,
> And country roads.
> How can it be possible?
And even more, I'm told I shall not be a sightseer or a
visitor, but an honored guest at a great wedding feast;
later to be given a new home where I may abide eternally.
There will be no sorrow there and no more night.
Can such wonders be for me?
> They say the price has been paid;
> That it is a gift of love;
> My mind can scarcely comprehend it—
But my spirit reaches out eagerly to receive it.
So tell me the story again and again; The story they call
HIS-STORY!

Wedding Bells
The Author's Story

It was the fourth of February, 1928, and a wedding was planned at the home of George and Fanny Bundy. It was the wedding of their youngest son, Vern, to Rosalind Batterbee, oldest daughter of Harry and Celesta Batterbee.

Both Vern and I were born and reared in nearby communities and although we moved several times over the years going as far as Flint and Lansing, we found there was no place like home and finally settled in 1942 on the farm in Jordan township where we now live.

God has blessed us with seven children, five of whom are living. Our oldest son Donald is married with two sons and two daughters and is a minister affiliated with the Free Methodist Church, serving in the Midwest.

Our two older daughters, Justine and Ardith, have married and have presented us with nine grandchildren. We also have a son, Robert, who has nearly completed his four years of service in the Air force, and a daughter nine years old, who is still at home.

Our home sits at the foot of Mt. Bliss, the hill that was named many years ago by the children of the district with their teacher and the community. It was dedicated to a well known hymn writer, P.P. Bliss, who wrote many of our best loved hymns.

At one time Mt. Bliss was noted on our Michigan maps and it is one of the few places near here where one can find oak trees. In years past there was also a flowing well on the top of the hill. But lumbermen, while dynamiting stumps for a skid-way, covered and diverted the flow so that now it only appears as a spring on the side of the hill. It has long been in our minds to put picnic tables and an observation platform on top of the hill. Perhaps someday we may.

In this first issue of my column I would like to make you acquainted with the area from which I write. Its rolling landscape includes a highland district on either side with a long broad valley between. It reminds me of a gravy dish which was sent to me from Japan. There is no handle on it but rather, it has a lip on each end.

Highway M 66 comes in at one end of the bowl, and the new road skirts the hogs-back range of hills all the way along the west side of the valley, (or bowl) finally leaving at the north end and entering East Jordan in Charlevoix county. You can also turn right at Chestonia on old 66 and skirt the Bohemian hills on the eastern side of the bowl and come out at the northern lip into East Jordan.

The valley is about one mile wide at the widest point with the Jordan River flowing full length, and it has a very special beauty both during the growing season and in the fall when the hills glow with color and every road seems to call for exploration.

𝔑ews

After nearly two weeks of detouring around the Chestonia Bridge the job seems to be nearing completion at last, and already we can see what a big improvement it is going to be.

But most of the news around the neighborhood seems to be in nature itself—in the trembling of the new leaves and the beauty of the blossoms. Even the birds and animals are beginning to appear with their little new additions. One of the oddest I have seen is a young porcupine moving around in the underbrush.

Things Memories are Made Of

I wonder if there aren't a great many people who feel like the lady who wrote to me and said, *I love to think over the old days, although I prefer autos and electrical gadgets to the hard way of life.* We tend to look at the past through a romantic haze, but most of us prefer the modern way of living. That is not only natural; it is as it should be. After all, the real reason for the romantic haze is that we realize what our forebears were working for and how well they accomplished it. This is the way life is meant to be.

But when we look at an old atlas, meet some old friends or wake in the middle of the night, our thoughts often turn back to the sights and sounds we knew as a child.

Here are some of the things I see and hear:

A clear morning, and from miles away the sound of a camp horn or triangle calling the men to breakfast and the distant sound of chopping that precedes a high clear call of tim-berrr...

I see section after section of cut-over woodlands and everyone's cattle running loose in them—where many times I looked for hours before locating our own. I see those same stump pastures during mushroom season.

Then wherever the loggers had gone, there always seemed to be a few high limbless trees left behind which we called stubs, and nearly always after a thunderstorm we could see one or more of those old stubs blazing away into the night until finally they had all burned or rotted away.

I remember wading barefoot through several inches of black ashes and seeing nothing green in all the way—for a forest fire had raged through the country, leaving nothing but destruction in its wake?

One of the clearest things I hear when I wake in the middle of the night is a train whistle, and a small thing like the fact that the train and track have been gone for many years doesn't seem to make much difference.

I think that is just about enough of my memories for now but I'm sure you have many memories of your own to keep you company in the night.

Have you ever sat down with an old atlas of our county (1910) and studied the old roads? Have you ever looked at the names on the old homesteads and tried to locate them on existing roads or to connect them with people now living? There is much mystery and romance right here in our own back yard if one has the patience to seek it out.

What adventures in home building the early settlers must have had, and where are they now? Some of those early pioneers are still around, and we have some newer neighbors as well—and some folks who are merely visitors. Would you like to meet a few of them through this column? You might even see someone from home.

Addendum

By the way, here is a little item that I learned as I poured over an old atlas.

There is one of our states that is divided into parishes instead of counties. Do you know which one it is?

School Days
And Green River's Early
Settlers

For a change of scenery this week I think I will move from Jordan Township to Chestonia and center around the Green River neighborhood. I will wander through the yesterdays, recalling a few names here and there that may bring back a memory or two.

I am thinking first of the district school where I put in many a day at what I thought pretty hard work. But we had our fun and days of excitement too for a little thing could keep the school buzzing all day.

There was the day Rachel Lifer broke her leg while playing Anti-I-Over and the day Joe Miller cut his finger off on the buzz saw and the teacher was called to help. Then there was the day that the Stickney house caught fire and we formed a bucket brigade to fight the flames—and, oh yes, the day my six year old brother, Bob, swallowed a four inch indelible pencil which frightened the teacher nearly to death.

There are sadder memories too, like those of war time when we stopped singing Kaiser Bill to hear that one of our schoolmate's brothers was being sent home for burial.

And the flu epidemic when everyone was sick and the Joe Elam family of seven was wiped out excepting for Joe and one daughter, Mildred. Not long after that a tree fell on Joe, killing him outright. I still wonder if tragedy has continued to follow Mildred.

Another event that I will never forget is the Sunday school that was held in the schoolhouse every Sunday rain or shine. I can still picture Mr. Burkholder driving up with his sedate team of grays hitched to his surrey with the fringe on top and Glen Brydon coming from the other direction in his open buggy with the high stepping bays.

Then when we got inside, Mr. Burkholder acted as our song leader. Even then his hand trembled so badly as he held his book that I used to wonder how he could read the words at all. But his voice was strong and true and he sang with a fervor that touched us all.

I remember Mrs. John Blaksley who played the organ; I can still see the way she used to pump the pedal so very hard when she was helping us, as children, to practice singing. Or if our voices grew weak during a program, she would sing, "la-la-la," at the top of her voice to help us out.

Do you remember the first evangelist you ever heard? I remember a man named Frank Smith, who made the rounds of all the lumbering districts, preaching the Word with great perseverance and dedication. I think I was about nine years old when he came to our schoolhouse. I sat in a seat near the front and trembled as the words seemed to come alive. The impression he made has never left me.

There are many things I could add to this list, but perhaps I have touched on a subject of interest to you or reminded you of a friend. I hope so, and that you will read my column again next week.

Pioneer Patter

Although I haven't a personal subject for my chat this week I am so immersed in the subject of pioneers in general that I think I will use just that. I have intensely enjoyed the hours spent poring over old books and listening to tales told by some of the remaining members of a generation that is nearly gone. I would love to be able to write these stories down in some permanent form. If I could write such a book I would call it "Pioneer Potpourri" for the condensation of so many stories would be like the jar my mother used to have, sweet and spicy. I remember one had only to lift the lid to be carried away on the wings of a strong, sweet odor.

A book could be like that, but it would take a greater talent than mine to bring out the greatness of their lives, for they were, on the whole, a plain people living a simple life and enjoying simple pleasures. Living conditions were not easy and many died in the conquest of the land, only to become the bridge for another, for they all had one thing in common. They were people with a vision.

Out of sight and seldom thought of, these pioneers are perhaps less appreciated than they deserve, or possibly they are more often thought of "in a lump" as it were, but I should like to get the jar and take out the petals one by one that I might better appreciate the beauty and sweetness of each one.

Delving into pioneer life makes you feel the emotions of a poet. It gives you the encompassing view of the novelist and a fervor for facts of the historian. Many stories still live in the hearts of those who remember the thrill and the labor of hewing a home out of the wilderness.

Though many of the early settlers' names are forgotten, we still see their homes here and there. We look at the site and think of all they endured so that we might live in comparative luxury. We can't help feeling an almost reverent respect, wondering how we might answer if one of those hardy fathers could speak to us and ask what we are doing that is worthwhile. Personally, in the light of what they have done, I would be ashamed to submit any of my accomplishments so far.

Nevertheless, something tells me that some hardy one would say, "Just do the best you can and never say die 'til you're dead."

How can we, with our eight hour day, with the utilities in the home, the ease of travel and communication, with the proximity of towns and medical aid and with safety at new high levels even begin to understand and picture life as the pioneers lived it?

There are hundreds of pioneer stories out there, simply withering away for lack of someone to preserve them. I would like to write such a book that would bring those stories to life. But realizing my shortcomings, I can only hope that someone will do it before all of our older residents have gone, taking with them the mysteries and adventures of their lives and sealing them forever in the yesterdays.

News

Such weather! I'm afraid the woodchuck we saw making forages back and forth across the field in front of our window Monday will decide he has made a mistake after all and crawl back in for another nap.

Second degree burns were suffered by the infant son of our Ex. Club demonstration agent, Mrs. Emma Reinbold, resulting in Ex. club shirt lessons postponement.

Sunbeam Ex. club held a recreation meeting at Mrs. Vern Bundy's Wednesday, honoring the birthdays of Mrs. Eva Hitchcock and Mrs. Ford Johnson. All members were present and gifts were given with games and a lunch of Jell-O, cake and coffee.

In town Tuesday I couldn't help but notice that Jordan Township is well represented in the line-up waiting for unemployment checks. Let's hope Mt. Clemens goes back to work soon.

Mires and Kocher Families

One of the few people living in our community today whose authority is recognized when it comes to the early lumbering era and coinciding events is Mr. Jim Mires of Chestonia. So many people have referred to him for particulars that it occurred to me that he himself would undoubtedly make an outstanding subject for review. I hope you will enjoy his story as much as I.

In the 1800s the population in Jordan Township was small and concentrated largely in comparatively small areas. One such area was on the north side of the Jordan Valley near East Jordan, and the other on the southern side near the heads of both the Jordan and Green rivers.

Between these two extremes of the township lay mile after mile of big trees. The railroad between Bellaire and East Jordan had not been built and Chestonia had not come into existence, but it was during this time that two families settled on and near what is now known as Chestonia hill.

One of these was J.B. Kocher, who became one of the first men to take interest, and hold office in the civic affairs of the township. The other was Mr. Mires, father of the subject of this review. Mr. Mires filed for his homestead at the foot, and in the shelter, of a big hill.

Kocher, when he arrived, preferred the fresh air and the good view to be had on the hilltop, so the two families filed on adjoining homesteads and became close neighbors.

Kocher was a farmer who had come from Ohio and settled about a half mile from the site where he finally built a permanent home eleven years later. If some of you who know the area have noticed a black walnut tree growing near the road at the site, look at it again when you pass and remember that the tree grew from a nut that was carried here from Ohio. It came in the pocket of a grandmother who hoped to bring one of the luxuries of her old home to this new land. It was her gift to her grandchildren—a gift that will keep on giving for many years.

Jim, who was only a few months old, when his parents arrived here, learned to know the surrounding woodlands as well as we know our back yards. He and a younger brother, Frank, thrived on the simple fare of the country and followed in their father's footsteps, as he cleared land, broke ground and planted crops. Jim's father and his boys after him hunted the hills for small game which gave both a variety to their menu and a welcome relief from the back breaking labor known by all pioneers.

Happily for Jim and Frank, the Kochers also had children and, growing up together, they learned how to keep their sense of direction in the woods and to differentiate between the maple and the elm tree. Many of the fruits of the land found their way into the family larders as they learned where to find each edible berry in its season and where the fish were likely to hide out in the heat of the day!

But all knowledge can not be obtained from Mother Nature, and when a school was built near Pinney Bridge, with Mrs. Pinney in charge, Jim and Arthur and Alice Kocher were enrolled.

Each day the children walked the ridges to school. Many times in the winter the snow was hip deep and during summer months they had to keep a sharp look out, as an occasional bear was seen. On these occasions they lost little time finding the nearest place of safety.

But these were not unusual conditions for the times and school went on. It was just one of those things, it seems. Cold winds or deep drifts—nothing seemed to hold terror for the sons and daughters of our pioneers.

The next few years they studied under several teachers, including Ida Pinney, Mattie Kearns, and never to be forgotten, Nellie McEwen. Sometimes the old call of the woods and the leaves under their feet made it very hard to sit in school, so one time when the teacher was out of the room, Jim, Arthur and Alice climbed out a back window and skipped for home. It was a big thrill until they began to wonder what to tell the teacher. It was finally settled to tell her that their cows had strayed near the school house and they had gone to take them home.

Of course the teacher's raised eye brows left little doubt as to whether she believed the tale, but she did let them get by with it. And the adventure left them with a secret that brought a chuckle or a hearty laugh when the event came to mind—though their glee was mixed with a feeling of guilt.

Jim was ever full of mischief which sometimes stretched his teacher's patience to the breaking point. And Nellie McEwen had about reached that point one spring day when, as all tried and true punishments had been to no avail, she was seeking a new approach. Suddenly Nellie's attention was attracted to the huge round oak heater which stood empty and cold in the center of the school room.

It was inspiration that prompted her then. She told Jim that she could see no other way than to shut him up in the big stove. The sight of the big black interior was too much for Jim, and as she struggled to get him into the heater, he decided that anything was preferable to that indignity. He humbly promised complete obedience to her rules. This meekness could not last, though it earned his freedom for a time. As Jim said, "It couldn't last, and the time came when I had to learn the hard way."

Jim outgrew the grade school and the punishments meted out for his boundless energy and his bent for leading others into mischief with him. But he never outgrew the energy or the ability to lead. And these, coupled with the knowledge and love of the woods, which he had learned as naturally as he learned to walk, combined to make him a natural woodsman at a time when woodsmen were most needed.

The greater part of Jim Mires life has been spent working in the forests of Antrim County and he has had a part in most of the major road and railroad projects. Another column will tell you some of his experiences on those jobs.

Forest Fires, Flu Epidemic and Other Hazards

Recalled by Jordan Township Lumberman

In 1898, the first railroad in the area was completed, and in 1899 a spur was laid through the Lilak Farm to another logging camp. Great gaps began to appear in the woods and the cry of "tim-berrr ..." rang throughout the area. The sound of camp horns and triangles dominated the one-time quiet of the deep woods.

At that time, when those first jobs started in the northern part of Jordan Township, Jim Myers was old enough to work in the camps and nothing could have kept him from it. From his first job on Willowbrook Farm (the old Mayhew place) he loved it.

Jim worked through 1913 and '14 as a log scaler, and from then on he ran his own camps. For many years he handled railroad jobs, logging operations or wood-camps, following the industry as the time or situation required. When asked about the nationality, ability and behavior of transient lumberjacks, Jim told me he had hired a great many of them for they filled a real need. Most common nationalities were Indian, Swedish and Polish with the greatest numbers being Indian. These he preferred above all others as they were the best all around workers and easiest to handle.

Jim must have handled his men well too, because he says he never had any trouble in his camps. He only remembers one serious fight in all his years of running camps.

Fires were one of the big hazards and Jim remembers several of quite menacing proportions. While working at Camp 9 on a road building operation, his crew was involved with a bad one which burned over thousands of acres. The company spent $1600.00 fighting the fire besides throwing all the men and equipment available into the fight.

Then in 1930 at another camp the jacks were alerted to the advance of a big fire. Thinking there was plenty of time, they towed their car camps across the creek for safety only to have the fire pass over the original site, jump the creek, and burn all the car camps to the ground.

But fires were only one of the many difficulties that faced those early woodsmen. During the epidemic of 1918, when the flu germ seemed to be everywhere and people were dropping off like flies, it was a hard time in the camps. People were so close together that isolation was next to impossible, and the few doctors available were busy in more populated areas. And to make matters worse, transportation on those old country roads was so slow that many died without medical attention.

Jim was running Camp 5 at the time and one of the things he remembers is how two of his men, who were sworn enemies and whose chief enjoyment was to spite each other, both fell victim to the flu, along with their wives and most, if not all, of their children.

Then in 1927, when the log camp was set up on Section 27 to take off the last of the virgin timber in Antrim County, Jim was there. And he must have remembered that first logging camp and marveled at the changing face of the country. I think it must have made him a little sad too, as he thought back to the time of his boyhood and the beauty of the untamed forest.

In 1929 Jim took a logging job across the Straits, but he was not used to the careless methods and inconsideration of the company for their men, and at the first opportunity he returned to Antrim County. The big jobs here were all finished, but there would be many smaller jobs in the second growth that was already beginning to appear. In between jobs, he could work on roads or do some of the many things he had always wanted to do.

At present Mr. Myers lives in a log cabin he built not far from his old home at Chestonia. Low and rambling, it has plenty of room and is as pleasant and comfortable a home as anyone could desire. He has a nice garden and always finds plenty to do.

Mr. Myers enjoys a good visit with old or new friends, but mostly he has his little terrier dog to keep him company.

If you are interested in stories of olden times, drop in on him some time. Perhaps he will tell you a lumberman's tale of how he and his brothers decided to spend the night in the upstairs of an old deserted homestead near Pinney Bridge—and how they spent most of the night killing porcupines on the stairs. But whatever the subject, you will find it interesting, for Mr. Myers at 77 has a clear memory and a keen sense of humor. And he somehow has you entering into the pleasure he plainly feels, whenever he looks back at his early experiences.

McGeesee County

You probably know that the country around Mancelona, Bellaire and East Jordan was settled quite a little ahead of the areas located between these towns, but did you know that when these towns were being settled, in about 1840, the surrounding land especially north of Mancelona toward East Jordan, was known as McGeesee County?

This name was on records until 1875 when Jordan Township was organized and the name officially changed.

I have no record of Chestonia Township but it must have been later, as the book I have on Northern Michigan Pioneers has no mention of it. Although there are a number of pioneer families recorded in that township.

By 1867 the villages were established and people were moving out from them in all directions wherever they could find a desirable location.

At this time a man named William Joquay established a homestead on land later included in Jordan Township. He was the first man to fall a tree in this area so to him goes the title of Jordan Township's first pioneer. Perhaps sometime I may be able to tell his story.

In reference to last week's pioneer story I want to say that I was most happy to receive a letter from Mrs. Ida Marchbanks, formerly Miss Ida Eby, who lived nearby and was acquainted with the family featured in the story.

Her letter gave a picture of the life of young people of that day, which I shall cherish. It took on a reality which I find most difficult to approach because it was told by one who lived it. I would be happy to hear from others who would like to write.

News

I have a report that an arctic owl was seen near here Thursday morning. I guess that means the winter was pretty hard farther north. All I know is that if I'd had his wings I'd have kept on going.

The ladies club of North Echo Township is sponsoring a drive for funds to erect a permanent memorial to the war veterans of this area. It is to be erected in East Jordan. It will be ten feet long seven feet high and there will be some eight hundred names engraved on metal and covered with glass. A Memorial Day dedication is planned.

Hitchcock: A Mushroom Town

Once again we are trying to pull back the curtains of obscurity so that we may see a little of the past. Though some may have heard about Hitchcock, there are not too many who have seen it as it is today. And I suppose that the people who lived there had as much hope of becoming a permanent town as any of the several other settlements of the time. Some of those old towns did survive, while others, like Hitchcock, have long ago surrendered their place on the map.

But a few do remember, and I think there are others who might be interested in their stories. For the story about Hitchcock I am indebted to Jim Mires of Chestonia.

The location is about one mile inland in Kearny Township from the corner where Star, Jordan and Chestonia lines come together. Or about five miles south of Chestonia by way of the EJ & S Railroad. The timber consisted mostly of hardwoods—maple, elm, birch, ash, hemlock and also some basswood. Lying near the railroad that ran between East Jordan and Bellaire, it was one of the earlier spots to be logged.

In 1900 when the lumber company arrived, they sought the best available camp site. They chose a hill which had at one time been homesteaded by a man named Brown. Mr. Brown, it is believed, retired to Bellaire to run a meat market.

Camp 10 was set up with Fred Larson as foreman and Mrs. Walt Pierce as cook. There were about sixty men quartered in the camp buildings and ten teams of horses, besides the families who moved into about ten separate houses. There was also a general store, blacksmith shop and school that doubled as a church on Sunday.

The store handled groceries, clothing and other necessities as well as dispensing the mail that was delivered daily by the EJ & S Railroad. The man who ran the store was named Hitchcock and his name was given to the settlement and put on the map.

The land was rolling but not a bad place to log and the timber held for five years.

The logs were hauled to the railroad on sleighs during the winter and the big wheels took over in summer. In places where logs were close to the railroad they were skidded to the track and loaded with a cross-haul. Dick Kallyshaw, who drove the cross-haul team, was killed as he was hooking the toggle chain. A log rocked onto him.

Another of the fatalities in this camp was caused by a swinging limb. Haliver (Handskipe) Peterson was felling trees when a limb came down out of a tree and hit him on the head.

Sometimes in logging these big trees the men came upon a limb that was broken and dangling, caused perhaps by the wind or by another tree falling into it. These swinging limbs were known by lumberjacks far and near as "widow-makers" for they could swing freely in almost any direction, killing a man at a moment's notice.

Still, when you consider the length of time on this job, the toll in lives was small for this hazardous occupation. Mostly the work went well and it was a happy camp. The daily work of logging went on; logs were cut, hauled, skidded and loaded. The best of the rock-elm was taken over by the square timber men and hewed into square timbers for special uses.

Lower Hitchcock

About 1903 when the bigger timber began to thin out, another camp was set up to take out cedar, and by 1905 the main camp was moved to a lower site a short distance away. This camp was known as Camp 2 of Lower Hitchcock. Dick Freeman took over the foreman's job for a time and was followed by Elmer Place.

Probably the accident most remembered is one involving twenty two cars which had been hauled onto a side track at the top of a two mile grade for loading. The brakeman was new and made the mistake of getting the brakes on only some of the cars and then uncoupling the engine.

The cars started rolling back and ran down the grade about a mile. Then they jumped the track and landed in a pile twenty feet high. Many of you will remember the picture of this wreck, which hung in the company store for years.

Lower Hitchcock never acquired the size of Upper Hitchcock, but there were several families, a store and a water tank to supply the railroad engines. Water was piped a quarter of a mile through the woods from a spot where they had dammed up a spring and laid two inch feeder pipe to the water tanks.

One of the men who ran the store in Lower Hitchcock was Steve Isaman. The last one was Earl Hagen in 1909. The mushroom season was over and the first fruits of Hitchcock's natural resources had been plucked, but in their place rose a more permanent development—a model farm that has kept the name alive not for nine years but for nearly half a century.

John Jones' Dream

This week I am starting a story of three generations—a combination of pioneer and modern history. It is the story of a farm, but first of all it is the story of a dream.

The dream was still there that night in March of 1900 as fatigue and cold bored into John H. Jones consciousness, making it hard to remember. It was easier if he thought back to his wife and two girls whom he had left behind in New York State and who were to follow him later.

John had bought this new home "sight unseen." He had started early that morning from the siding at Simons where they had unloaded his stock and furniture, and though the trail may have been easy to follow in summer, it was an unbroken path now. His team had struggled valiantly all day through the snowbound trail, plodding along where the snow was shallow. Lunging desperately through the drifts, they were fast reaching the limit of their endurance.

Just now the going was hard, it was uphill and the load was heavy. Perhaps John had been foolish to buy a farm he had never seen and that was hundreds of miles away in such raw and unsettled country.

When John reached the top of the hill, he would look around for a suitable place to spend the night, and if there was no shelter, he might use his ax to peel long strips of bark from the trees to make one. In those last moments before he reached the top he thought once more of his farm, and the trees and snow faded away. In their place he saw the hills and valleys covered with green pastures that were dotted with cattle and a big dairy barn off to one side. Oh, if only his farm could be all he hoped and prayed!

Then as the team finally reached the top of the hill, John looked down at a logging team traveling a path that was definitely a road. He realized he was nearing his destination. No highway had ever looked so good!

Even the team seemed to realize that relief was near. They pricked their ears and stumbled eagerly down the hill.

On reaching the road, John hurried along and soon found a settler's cabin, where he was welcomed for the night. The settler's name was Pinney and he knew well the farm John had bought.

That night John talked to Mr. Pinney about the farm he had purchased, eager to learn first hand all about the place.

The next morning, after a good night's rest and a warm meal, things looked much brighter. John went on his way with new zeal and determination.

Later, as John stood looking down on his new home, his doubts of the night before vanished into the air. John put up the stock and unloaded the household goods before he settled down by a warm fire, and all the problems and setbacks seemed to blend into a realization of final accomplishment. The first hurdle had been conquered and somehow at that moment John had an assurance that he would see the rest of his dream fulfilled as well.

Through the years John never lost sight of his dream and little by little he built the farm, clearing the land, tilling it and planting nearly every variety of fruit. He found the land fertile, and because it was on high ground, it had unusual freedom from frost for this part of the country.

In time John's daughters became adults and married. One of them moved away, but the other, Louanna, married a neighbor, Ernest Williams. In 1903 Louanna and Ernest began their married life in her parents' home, and it was there that their only child, Lorena, was born. Lorena grew and became a school teacher adding one more link in the chain that was John Jones' dream.

Lorena

During the four years that Lorena Williams taught at the Simons School, she met and married Art Morris. Art was the son of Alonzo Morris, and their farm was just four and a half miles north of Alba.

After the marriage, Art and Lorena moved in with her grandfather, John Jones—a perfect arrangement for John, because Art became the son he had never had. Art entered into John Jones' dream with his whole heart, and while Mr. Jones' health held up, the farm prospered as never before. The herds increased and at last in 1939 John built his dairy barn. The dream was complete.

Due to an injury sustained in a fall from an apple tree, Mr. Jones's ability to walk during his last years was limited by the use of two canes. He spent his winters with his daughter who lived in the city, but when summer came, he returned to the farm, the site of his dream. I like to think of Grandfather Jones sitting in a chair on his hilltop, looking down on his green fields all dotted with yellow and white guernseys and with his fine dairy barn standing in grand array off to one side. And while he sat enjoying the view, his three grandchildren, sandy haired Fern and twins, Delwin and Darwin, played around his knees. Delwin and Darwin, small replicas of their father, were the fourth generation to live in that old farmhouse.

Grandfather Jones passed away in 1945 during the war years when there was a shortage of teachers. Mrs. Lorenea Morris taught at the Rockery School for a year before the community decided the school was too small and moved the children to the consolidated school at East Jordan.

Meanwhile the children were growing and time seemed to fly. A day came that Fern had graduated from high school. She tried college but was forced to give it up because of illness. Later she joined the Navy and served three years in Memphis, Tennessee. She mustered out in 1952 just as her brothers' entered the service.

They served with the Army Security branch in Southern Bavaria. All three children are home now and each is holding down a job.

They use their spare time to help their father, who now has thirty five fine Guernsey cows in John Jones' dairy barn. Art Morris does his routine chores using his Surge Milker, of which he is an ardent advocate.

During all these years Art and Rena have taken a very special interest in keeping the Sunday school in the community alive. They spared no trouble and at all times they set a good example of Christian living before their children and the community.

Addendum

One of Jordan Township's first residences melted to the ground on a Sunday morning, when the home of

Mr. and Mrs. Art Morris went up in flames. The house was built by the man who first homesteaded the place in the 1800's.

Taken over in 1900 by John Jones, it has been in almost constant residence ever since sheltering his family over five generations.

At one time this house was a part of a good sized community chosen by the first English speaking settlers of Jordan Township. Many of the early families settled originally in Rockery and the community school was always known by that name.

In the years since much of the community has shifted nearer town. People have moved, passed away or rebuilt. Few of the early families remain and one by one the old residences have burned, until now the Calkins house is the only one left. It sits like a lone soldier, left standing alone on the field.

It was 2:00 AM, when Mrs. Morris was roused from her sleep by a noise she took to be a motor running. She rose, turned on the light and found the outer rooms in flames. All of the six people who were sleeping in the house escaped unharmed and most of the dining and front room furniture was saved. Overall loss has not been established but it is partially covered by insurance. The most immediate needs are cooking utensils. If you would like to help, I suggest "a pan and a pound."

Mr. and Mrs. Marty Denhammer of Battle Creek have opened their cottage for the family's use until other arrangements can be made.

News

Tragedy struck in our neighborhood again Wednesday afternoon when Bert Mayhew committed suicide at his home. He was found by a neighbor, Mr. Austin, who found a note that Mr. Mayhew had left. Mr. Austin found Bert behind his barn where he had shot himself with his 30:06 rifle. No reason for his act has yet been made public.

Maple Syrup "The Way It Was"

Having not quite finished my "story of the week," I think I will fall back on the history of a subject which is always appropriate at this time of year. I am speaking, of course, of the time honored custom of making maple syrup.

I remember as a girl, visiting a sugar house and watching the process of boiling down the barrels of what appeared to be water but was really maple sap until they became, in the finished product, a delicacy of inimitable flavor. As a teenager I once attended a "sugaring off" party where the syrup was boiled down to a solid and this also was an unforgettable treat.

As I grew older, I often wondered why so few people took advantage of this opportunity which flows so freely every spring, and finally, when my own boys were grown, I had my opportunity.

It didn't take much urging to get my son Bob to hitch up a horse and dray and transport the big black kettle, chains, spiles and pails over the hill and into a small valley. From this central position he could reach a number of sizable maple trees on the hillsides all around him.

After building a tripod large enough to swing the kettle and to have a good fire beneath, he set up the fire shields and started tapping the trees. The trees were obliging and the sap was soon dripping and running merrily into the pails.

From that time on Bob was running too. It took all his daylight hours to carry the sap and cut wood to keep the fire going. We soon found that "sap was a-wastin'" if the fire was not kept constant day and night.

Sleep was a thing one did between piling on wood and pouring and stirring and skimming.

Seeing how tired he looked, I took one of the girls one night and we took a turn at it. I waded along the narrow passageways through the snow and fumbled in the dark for the full sap pails. When finally I finished carrying sap, I piled some of the wood he had left for me to use on the fire. Then I sat down near it.

The fire felt fine in front, but I soon found it a simple matter to broil on one side and freeze the other at the same time. It was either that or keep moving. I kept moving!!—not only turning first my face and then my back to the heat but also moving from side to side to escape the gushes of smoke which shifted with the wind every few minutes.

By morning my pioneer instincts were as smoked and dried as pemmican, and I had a much greater respect for those who produce maple syrup in quantities. I no longer wonder why it is so expensive, and I have gotten a few facts together about it. I hope you will find them interesting.

According to legend, Moqua, an Indian squaw became so engrossed in her embroidery she forgot the moose meat she was cooking in maple sap outside the wigwam. When the chief returned, he found a new wonderful food waiting. His meat was surrounded by a thick brown syrup. He was delighted and informed his tribe that Kose-Kusbek had shown Moqua directly from heaven how to make syrup by boiling sap.

Soon many Indians profited by her mistake. Using tomahawks and stone axes, they inserted a piece of bark or a reed to convey sap into a container.

These receptacles were made of birch bark or the bark of elms. After they were filled, the Indians emptied them into a trough made of a hollow log. Then they heated stones to put in it until the syrup was ready.

Pioneers quickly learned to make syrup too. It was a great boon to their scanty larder. They called it Indian sugar and Indian molasses. They used wooden spouts rather than reeds and caught the sap in buckets. Then they boiled it in iron kettles.

Nowadays methods are even more improved, but the old maple trees are still rendering sap for our use. Trees have been found with evidence that they had been gashed with Indian axes, bored with augers of pioneers and in their last days tapped by the smaller augers and bits that are used today.

There are some 70 varieties of maple in the world. Of these the sugar maple, or rock maple as it is sometimes known, and the black maple produce the best sap for making syrup and sugar. It takes from one to two barrels of sap to make a gallon of syrup, depending on the varying sweetness of the sap.

The syrup produced by the Indians was dark and impure, but they used it to some extent for barter. The pioneers, with a better grade of syrup, were able and glad to store it for future use.

Today all maple syrup is required by law to weigh eleven lbs. to the gallon. The best grade is yellowish amber in color and delicately flavored. It is a purely American product that has been described as "an unadorned, unadulterated product that fills a niche of its own, and can be made by any American housewife in any kitchen in the land."

Maple syrup has been a staff and a crutch—yes even life itself, to our ancestors. In better times it has become an industry and a "must" as an accompaniment of our favorite griddle cakes. In its concentrated form it is a confection.

Just one more observation, as a youngster, I remember my mother making maple syrup in her kitchen. True she used only part sap and hurried it up with sugar, but one touch she added that I have failed to find anywhere else, and that was accomplished by taking a suitable amount of chips from the bark of a maple tree and sewing it into a bag. Then she boiled it with the sap. Mmmmmm! Delicious!

It makes one think that Chief Woksis was right. It surely was a gift from heaven.

David Rainey and the Stone House

For as long as I have lived in this community I have been aware of an old homestead which seems to hold a special attraction for children. Perhaps it is because the house has survived the elements a little better than most, but I think it is largely because of the variety of things that grow there. There seems to be something to reap at nearly every season of the year and so it is the target of a great many of the children's expectations.

In spring they are likely to find a bouquet of daffodils or an armful of lilacs. A little later it will be roses or early apples. In the fall it may still be apples or perhaps some grapes. But whatever the children find, they always return home tired but happy and filled to bursting with the excitement of their day.

The house itself could be called a landmark of the community, as it is visible from the road—although there is no longer a road to its door. It is in reality the old David Rainey farm, but because it is built of fieldstone it is known to the neighborhood children simply as "The Stone House."

The house has stood empty for many years and although most of the walls and roof are still intact, the windows are gone and the doors no longer close. Consequently the beautiful woodwork that once adorned the interior has been suffering grievous assault by porcupines for some years now.

A few years ago, during the war and after learning the owner lived in East Jordan, I went to see her to try and buy the woodwork. Lumber was almost impossible to buy at the time and it seemed a shame to see that beautiful woodwork being carried away by mouthfuls.

But although the owner was quite willing to sell the farm for a small sum providing the home was restored and used, she could not bring herself to sell a stick to be torn out and taken away.

"It was a wonderful home once," she told me. "It was almost like heaven to us children." And she went on to tell me that the whole place, both the stone and the lumber, had been built with materials taken from the farm itself, and largely by her father's own hands.

David Rainey was born and raised in Antrim County, Ireland. He got his schooling there and then joined the British Navy where he served only a short time. After leaving Britain to join the U.S. Navy he served through the War of the Rebellion and then sailed the Great Lakes. In time he homesteaded a place in Antrim County, which is now Jordan Township.

David included all of the feasible branches of farming in his operation, giving special attention to the raising of poultry and production of honey. He also raised livestock and cultivated a very productive orchard. During this time he met and married Miss June Orman, with whom he had four children.

The old home is nearly gone now and very few of the neighbors who are here ever knew Mr. and Mrs. Rainey. But for the Rainey children, David and

June, it made a wilderness home to remember. It was a paradise where they were surrounded by flowers and lived on fruit and bread and honey in a veritable Canaan.

Perhaps a little of their happiness still lingers in the atmosphere for it attracts the children who go there to play. The home may be gone and the farm now just idle ground but who can say their lives were spent in vain?

The Other Side of the Coin

In the year of 1869 in the upper part of Michigan's Lower Peninsula the Jordan River flowed through Antrim County even as it does now, but the hills and valleys it bisected were strangely different for the fields, pastures and hills of the present were covered with huge virgin pine and hardwoods. These sloped off to a softer aspen and birch with stretches of low ground and almost impassable swamps.

This is an authentic story of the early days when the country was new and men who came from many countries for many reasons learned to love the land and remained to live, to build and to cherish it as their own.

On this day in May the bushes bordering the river parted and a short broad shouldered man pushed through them backward, dragging a rude boat up onto the river bank.

Timothy Ryan moved swiftly. Taking an ax from the bottom of the boat, he removed the rest of his gear and turned the boat upside down among the bushes.

To finish the job he cut a few branches and placed them carefully over the boat until it was completely hidden with no broken ends to attract attention.

When this was finished, he shoved the axe handle through the pack strap and boosted it to his shoulders.

Shifting the load till it sat comfortably, he picked up his long rifle. After one keen glance toward the boat and another that swept the surrounding country he started off on the faint trail leading upgrade into the timberland.

As Timothy was plodding along the winding trail, the balmy spring day became warmer and his naturally ruddy complexion became even redder. The spattering of freckles on his face took on more color too and the perspiration gathered in beads on his brow, trickling down the sides of his face.

But minor discomforts couldn't discourage this man for his eyes and heart were filled with the beauty and promise of abundance he saw around him. Timothy admired the majestic hardwoods nodding their leafy crowns on the hill knowing that when winter came, he would find big squirrels nesting there.

As he moved up the valley, the cedars gradually gave way to pine. The occasional miry spots and quavering sods became a thick carpet that gave under foot like an expensive rug, and the scent of pine needles that were both overhead and underfoot filled the air.

Tim was on rising ground now and his path led through a stand of aspen trees. It was so pleasant here that he decided to stop for lunch and a short rest.

It was a relief to put down his load, and as he stood with his pack at his feet, he slowly massaged the tired aching muscles of his neck. His busy eyes were taking note of his surroundings.

The poplars branched off to one side so that Tim could see the glint of a small stream.

The ground was in good condition for a safe fire and a glance showed plenty of dry lower branches within easy reach that would make a quick hot fire.

By the time the fire was blazing, Tim had built a tripod of forked sticks. On this he hung a small pail of water that he had dipped from the clear stream. It didn't take long to brew a pail of good strong tea.

Timothy took his time at lunch sipping the tea gingerly, while he nibbled the hard biscuits from his pack. Finally he lay back on the sod with his arm over his eyes and drowsily listened to the pattering of aspen leaves overhead. He wondered how many times the native Indians had camped here and rested beneath the trees trying to understand their many voices. As he pondered, the patter of the leaves faded away to a murmur and he slept.

While the man slept, the woodland creatures grew courageous and soon went about their business as usual. Red squirrels and chipmunks did their early spring housecleaning and cottontails scurried about gathering dry grasses for the new families they expected soon.

A blue jay perched on a limb nearby and peered curiously at the man who was lying on the ground. Cocking his head first on one side and then the other, he seemed to miss nothing, from the rusty locks and rugged features to the rawhide strings dangling from the man's sturdy boot tops.

The rustle of leaves faded in Timothy Ryan's mind. In his dream he was a boy again, wandering the hills and valleys of his native Ireland. Now he was fishing the old trout stream dreaming of the day when he would be old enough to seek adventure on the high sea and to find a new life and fortune in a new land.

Suddenly disturbed, it seemed he no longer held a fishing pole but snares, and the drumming of a cock partridge was filling his ears. The partridge was still drumming as he opened his eyes. This!! This, he realized, is my new world.

The jay darted away with a startled cry.

Tim sat up, and drew up his knees. Wrapping his arms around them he sat drinking in the marvels of his new country.

He had settled, he thought, not for riches of gold but for the wealth of timber, good soil, teeming rivers and abundant forests.

He remembered his years in the English Navy and the many tales he'd heard about America and its brave, free men.

It had struck a cord of admiration in him even then. For here was a country that had succeeded in forcing its freedom, as his country had tried for so many years to do.

He too had longed to be free. And now, transplanted from Antrim County, Ireland to Antrim County Michigan, he had decided that here he could build his home. Yes, he would raise his family here and freedom would be the heritage of his children!

Brushing his hand across his eyes, Timothy came quickly to his feet. He would need all the remaining daylight hours to reach his homestead.

Tonight he would camp on the slope of the hill among the white birches and tomorrow he would start his new home.

Once more Tim shouldered his pack and courageously turned his face from the past and toward the future.

Behind him, from the ridge of the hill, a solitary Indian watched until he was out of sight. The Indian's face showed no expression, but when he turned to leave, his head was bowed and his step was not as silent as usual. As he walked away his moccasined feet left but a small impression on the woodland floor and this would soon fade away.

HONESTY

So much is meant by "Honesty!!"
New meanings oft' we find;
So many things included and so many things implied.
There's honesty of instincts and honest heart and mind,
And which is most important? It's a hard thing to
decide.

What do YOU mean by "Honesty?"
Do you dare to search your mind?
To find the inmost answer from an unknown deep?
Can you accept a truth, tho' others made the find?

Here is the test of "Honesty."
That gives the truth away,
A deceitful heart or twisted mind
Betray them selves, when "Instinct" holds its sway;
For integrity and truth, must spring
From the inmost heart of thine,
Then "Honesty' in HEART and MIND,
Shine through as light of day

Emma Shepard & Mushroom Village of Chestonia

Original Owner of Chestonia Store, Back in Early 1900's Is Present Operator

By 1905 Antrim county was considered settled and though much of Michigan's virgin forest was already gone, here in Antrim County there were still quite a few acres of the "big trees."

At first the settlers, in order to find room for their buildings, their gardens and their orchards had cut the big trees by hand. Burning them in big piles, they destroyed what in later years could have made them independently wealthy.

But what else could they do? They had to have a place for their families. There were no roads, no mills and no markets.

Often they used just the outer slabs with the bark attached to make their first rude homes. Later with more time they learned to hew the smaller logs, shaping and laying them one on another and using only wooden pins to hold them together. This made a comfortable home that lasted very well.

But by 1905 there were roads of a sort for transportation. There were saw mills and markets and though the price the settlers got for lumber would seem negligible now, it was life to many of the settlers.

The big lumber camps imported much of their help from among the local men, who farmed in summer and hewed the great trees in winter. These men of the lumber woods we knew as lumberjacks.

As financial circumstances improved and population increased, the demand for food, implements and comforts also increased. To meet this demand several small towns and villages sprang up in Antrim County. Chestonia, with its two blacksmith shops, a potato warehouse, a school and twenty shanties with families was a thriving community. There were also two railroad depots in the community, the D&C depot east of the present 66 highway and the EJ & S depot across the track from the present station and store. The E J & S depot also housed a grocery store, which was named the Davis store. It served as a post office where the mail was received each day from East Jordan and from Bellaire.

At this time a young couple, Homer Shepard and wife, Emma Valentine-Shepard, moved into the area from Barry County in Michigan and within the year they built the present store across the tracks from the E J & S and operated it for three years.

During that time their children, Vail, Marshall and Velma, were born and they decided to move to a farm. Mrs. Shepard's parents, Mr. and Mrs. Valentine, took over the store and operated it as long as they lived. But when Mrs. Shepard's mother passed away in 1935, leaving the store unattended,

Mrs. Shepard returned to the store having lost her husband in 1929.

Today the Shepard children are married and she is alone, but she continues to tend the store. She takes care of the customers herself and whether you want ten gallons of gas or a spool of thread, you get service with a smile.

Mrs. Shepard also has a very nicely furnished cabin which she rents. You might keep this in mind in case some of your friends would like a homelike place to spend their vacation.

Mary Fataj-Kortanek

In the early years of the settling of Jordan Township there began to appear quite a sprinkling of people from the country of Bohemia. Partly because they spoke a different language and partly because they were lovers of the land, they began to settle together in a part of the country suited to agriculture. This area became known as the "Bohemian Settlement" or "Bohemian Hills."

They were good farmers and soon a thriving farm community began to emerge from the wooded land. Relatives came from Bohemia to join these people and became an impregnated part of America and of our country.

I have long had a desire to tell the story of one of those early pioneers of the Settlement District, and this week I'm privileged to introduce you to Mary Fataj-Kortanek, a Bohemian settler who came to America alone, without family, at age fifteen and is still active in community affairs at age eighty one.

Mary Kortanek is undoubtedly very familiar to a great many people living around East Jordan, for she first came to this part of Michigan many years ago. And much of that time has been spent right here in the town of East Jordan.

Still many of you may not know her history, and I think her well deserving of special attention, especially at this time when the United States is accepting hundreds of foreign people into our land. It may reassure those who are a little apprehensive about the move to take a look at others who have borne the title of foreigners and been able to live and make places for themselves among us without the help that the present incoming groups receive.

Mary Fataj left Bohemia in 1891. She was fifteen at the time and she was leaving father, mother, sister and brothers to join an older sister in the United States. Traveling alone, except for friends, she finally reached Chicago. There she moved into her sister's home, where she helped with house keeping duties and found work helping in other homes as well.

At age twenty five, after ten years in Chicago, Mary met Josef Kortanek a young mill worker who was also a native of Bohemia. The attraction was mutual, and they were married on February 4, 1901. Mr. Kortanek worked in the mills until he joined his brother-in-law at the stock yards.

In time Mary's two brothers and one sister came to America from Bohemia, and the brothers found work in the stockyards. This proved to be a mistake, however, for it led to a tragic conclusion. Mary's older brother was killed by a descending elevator at only twenty one years of age.

Over the years the confining work at the stock yards began to break down Mr. Kortanek's health, and the Doctor ordered a move. Mary Kortanek found herself transported with her husband and five children from a bustling city with a regular income to a shanty, as she describes it, way back in the woods at East Jordan, Michigan. There Mr. Kortanek worked on the farms of his friends and in the lumber mills—a business he knew well.

But the contrast between life in Chicago and life in the woods was almost too much for Mary and from the first she hated it. She became so despondent she could no longer bear to write to her parents.

And when she finally found the courage to write, she had lost track of them and was never able to contact them again.

In time the Kortaneks made their final move into the outskirts of East Jordan. There they bought a small home on the Cooperage Road, and Mary Kortanek found a permanent job at the chemical plant.

The Kortaneks had three more children after coming to Michigan, two boys and six girls. One daughter was lost at the age of nine of typhoid fever. A son was lost at age nineteen.

Although Mary found life here not to her liking at first, she was too sensible not to make the best of it, and when Mr. Kortanek passed away in 1940 of a long standing organic ailment, Mary carried on the same as ever. She never spared herself but even raised two of her grandchildren as her own. Only one of Mary's six children lives nearby. The others live in Lansing, Detroit and Traverse City. The granddaughter she raised is happily married and the grandson is now in his second year of service in the Navy.

Although the desire of Mary's heart has long been to make a short visit to Chicago and the places she remembers, time has changed her feelings toward northern Michigan. It has become her home. She raised her family of eight children here. She has twenty two grandchildren and fifteen great grandchildren and is known as Grandma to many of the neighborhood children.

And she has kept her sense of humor, which is evident in her ready smile and the sparkle in her eye.

Now at eighty one years of age Mary's eyes are scarcely dimmed. She is one of the most active people for her age that I have ever seen. She makes the mile walk back and forth to town for groceries regularly. Being a devout Catholic, she often makes the long walk to early morning services, and she's likely to be on hand to lend support for others where it is needed.

Since Mary is alone she spends a lot of time at her hobby of rug making. She sells the rugs when she is able and also gives them as gifts to young couples whom she knows. Her home is full of the product of her hands. Crocheted articles and rugs share honors with African Violets and the pictures of her family that crowd the top of her piano.

Mrs. Kortanek may not have wealth untold but I think Mary Fataj has made a success of her life in a strange land. And I think the new ones who are coming into our country will do the same.

While we were visiting Mrs. Kortanek told me that her grandson who is in the Navy has written to ask for some of her Prune Biscuits—a specialty of hers that has long been a favorite of the young man. The topic gave me the idea that perhaps you would all enjoy a favorite recipe, if I could get one occasionally. Accordingly, I snapped this one up, and I hope those of you who are not acquainted with it will try it soon, they are delicious.

Prune Biscuits

These biscuits are made of a light bread dough. Be sure it is the type made with milk rather than all water, also using a little extra shortening.

While the yeast sponge is setting, cook about four cups of soaked prunes till soft, sweeten and add cinnamon and allspice to taste.

After dough has risen in the hard loaf and is ready for panning, cut off chunks the size of a small tangerine and flatten each one on the bread board. Then spoon a small amount of the cool prune paste on each one.

Gather up edges of each and pinch them together. Place in the pan with the pinched edges down. Let rise thirty minutes.

Save one back to eat with your coffee while you read your paper.

Pierre Raveau

Perhaps 1914 doesn't seem so long ago to us and perhaps we think of our country as pretty well settled and civilized at that time, but to Mr. and Mrs. Claude Raveau, farmers in the small village of Chaoreux, central France, America was a wild unsettled country teeming with Indians who were ready to scalp any unwary traveler.

And to make matters worse, their eighteen year old son, Pierre, was determined to go there. They bade him farewell, expecting never to see him again.

Pierre himself had an entirely different perspective. From childhood he had listened avidly to every scrap of information he could find about America. He had heard many lurid tales of the savagery of the Indians and the dangers of the uncivilized country, but he had also heard exciting accounts of gold to be scooped up by handfuls. And being not of a timid nature, he thought that it would be well worth the risk. Accordingly, he had started at age fifteen to save every franc he could get hold of to pay his passage to that new country.

The fund increased very slowly and by small amounts but by the time he was eighteen Pierre had at last reached the goal. His parents, who thought him quite out of his mind for taking such a chance, finally gave in to the inevitable and gave their consent.

As it turned out they never did see their son again, but it was not the dangers of the country that prevented it. He so fell in love with America that he could not be prevailed upon to return even for a short time.

It was not possible at that time for the young man to come straight to the United States. He had to have a sponsor and the sponsor he was assigned was a farmer by the name of Jauthier. Jauthier lived in Canada and that was a long way in the right direction, so Pierre didn't hesitate.

The trip to Canada was easy and uneventful and the Jauthiers were fine people. Before long Pierre became one of the family, along with a young orphan girl of fourteen named Berta Durand.

Berta had been one of a family of ten and had lost her mother when she was six months old. Then when she was nine her father died and she was placed in a convent school, where she stayed until the Jauthiers gave her a home.

Pierre lived with these good people for eight years, and in 1922 he moved to Florida. He had heard that it was a simple matter in Florida to obtain money, but after two months in Florida he decided that "all is not gold that glitters" and he came north to Detroit to work in a factory.

Pierre fared well in Detroit and about two years later he returned to Canada for a visit. He was now twenty eight years old and had made good use of his money. He dressed well and rode one of his three motorcycles.

He cut a dashing figure, and Berta was attracted at once, though she had paid him little serious attention before.

Berta also had blossomed into a desirable young woman and Pierre didn't fail to notice. With such a combination plus the knowledge they already had of each other, who could be surprised that romance would spring into full bloom?

After several trips back and forth between Canada and Detroit Pierre and Berta were married and settled in Detroit.

From the beginning Pierre had been fascinated by engines and anything that would run was of intense interest. There seemed to be an endless stream of vehicles passing through his hands. Even in the early years of the automobile he contrived to always have one of some sort to experiment with. His earliest was one of the old "Haroon's" of 1915 vintage.

It is still a subject of great amusement to Pierre and Berta that he seemed to have a different car each time he came to visit. One he especially remembers held together 'til he got there but had to be sold for bus fare to get back.

Mr. Raveau himself tells of one trip which took five days from Detroit to Montreal. He says it was because of the poor roads of that time.

The honeymoon chariot, which brought Pierre and Berta back to Detroit, was an Olds with a wooden body. Pierre is quick to point out that, "You can't hardly find none of them no more!!"

Pierre spent nineteen years in the factories of Detroit and by that time he and Berta were not two but a family of seven having become the proud parents of three boys and two girls. The war was over and industry had begun to relax its hold on the laboring man and that was all right with the Raveaus. They were beginning to look around for a farm, where they could relax from the long grind of shop work.

It was just luck that they happened to see an ad in a paper about a farm near Boyne City. It seemed to fit their needs and they made a trip to see it.

The farm was a disappointment to them but as they meandered around the country side, they were attracted to the area along highway 66. After some inquiries they bought the place where they now live.

The first few years were hard with lots of work to do and little money coming in. The Raveaus just buckled down and worked harder. Now they not only have a beautiful home but Pierre has a bump shop and a herd of about forty beef animals.

The children have grown and found lives of their own. The older son, John, spent two years in the navy and then he and Ramon, whom many of you know, moved to Detroit where John works in the factory and Ramon does carpentry.

The girls, Jackie and Teresa, are living in St Clair Shores, and between them they have presented Pierre and Berta with 6 grandchildren.

The youngest son, Jimmie, is still at home. He attends school and serves as his father's right hand man.

There is one other member of the family who has not been mentioned. Nine year old Dawn Hughey has been living in the Raveau household for a while now and already seems to have found a place in their hearts.

Both Pierre and Berta are members of the Catholic Church and enjoy worship. They hold memberships in the Farm Bureau Organization, and Berta takes part in several community clubs. Mrs. Raveau says she has no hobbies, but just judging from my visit in her home, I would say her hobby is "doing everything" and doing it "just a little better."

Mr. and Mrs. Raveau are very happy with their life here and although they hear occasionally from relatives in France, they have no desire to go back. This is their country—for keeps.

In accordance with my last story I asked Berta if she had a "different" recipe and she came up with a way to use extra pastry—left over or made especially. She had no name for it, but I call it Pastry Surprise Cookies.

Pastry Surprise Cookies

Step 1. Roll pastry to a VERY thin square.

Step 2. Spread half with a thin layer of your favorite filling—date, raisin, jam or jelly. All are good.

Step 3. Fold second half over top of filling.

Step 4. Prick top layer thoroughly to prevent air bubbles.

Step 5. Brush with milk and sprinkle heavily with sugar.

Step 6. Bake to a golden brown, cut in squares and cool.

Arnold Hart Family

Feeling that it is again time to recognize some of our present residents, I have decided to tell you the story of my neighbors, the Arnold Hart family. Arnold, Beatrice and their children have been Jordanites for about ten years and are probably known by many of you.

In 1902 when Arnold's parents, Abram and Theda Hart, moved from their farm in Ohio to the Traverse City area, Arnold was only five months old. Consequently he doesn't go into detail about the trip.

The fifth child in a family that later grew to the old fashioned number of ten, Arnold grew up pretty fast, and at the age of five he was going out early in the morning with the cattle. He kept the herd together all day and brought them home at night. At twelve he went to work as a flunky in a logging camp.

But Abram felt he had outgrown the farm at Cedar Run and in 1916 he took Arnold with him into the country near Gaylord. There he found land that suited him and he and Arnold spent the summer working the land. They built a barn, cleared some land, put up a little wild hay and raised potatoes before returning to Cedar Run to harvest grain and beans.

Perhaps the heavy schedule was too hard on Arnold, however, for when Abram was ready to return to Gaylord, Arnold had pneumonia. Nevertheless, Abram himself did go back. He took a team and worked at a logging camp all winter with Clayton Harder.

In June Abram was ready to move. He prepared the stock for travel along with the implements and sent them ahead by box car. Then Abram, Theda and nine children made the trip on the wagon with the household goods.

Over the next several days of travel the large family had quite an adventure. The trip was especially difficult for Arnold for he was still very ill, and barely able to ride.

Soon after the move to Gaylord Arnold took a job at Perrington in the Libby McNiel Condenserie, where he made friends with a young married couple named J.B. and Alice Bussler.

But Arnold was a restless individual whose great interest in life was to find what was around the next bend and over the next hill. He worked at one place just long enough to finance his travels and then moved on. So he soon lost track of his friends.

He never lost sight of home, however, for he made frequent returns to visit his family.

Then on one of his jaunts afield Arnold received the surprise of his life. While working with a threshing crew in the Dakotas, he approached the house for a drink of water or something. And when the door opened, he found it occupied by his old friends the Busslers. He visited a bit and then moved on.

From Dakota Arnold went to Canada to cut pulp, but he was not satisfied. He returned to Michigan and found work with George Cadwell on the Elmira Hill. It was at this time that he met Beatrice Sheaffer.

Beatrice was the daughter of Ben Sheaffer who operated a harness and shoe shop in Boyne City. She was also the fifth child in a family of ten and she was visiting a girlfriend in Gaylord. It turned out that she liked her girlfriend's boyfriend. And as it happened, the boyfriend liked the girl friend's girlfriend too. In August 1924 Beatrice and Arnold were married.

Over the next few years Arnold continued to travel, always trying for the gold ring on the merry-go-round. But farming seemed to hold a satisfaction that all other jobs lacked, and he always came back to it.

So in the end Arnold and Beatrice bought a farm near Gaylord.

Wanderlust prevailed, however, and the Harts moved about every two years. They made moves to Holland, Zeeland, Acme, Rapid City, Gaylord, Johannesburg and Muskegon.

At Holland their first child, whom they named Arnold after his father, was born. In Zeeland Arnold senior developed a chronic quinsy condition and was advised by a doctor to move to a rural district. They spent the summer at Acme, and then moved to Rapid City where their second son, Delbert, was born. From there they moved to Elmira where the stork dropped another bundle, a boy named Earl. They moved to Gaylord and the next bundle that came along answered to the name of Theda.

In 1939 they moved to a farm in Johannesburg and moved again in '42 to Muskegon where Arnold got a job with the Military Police. He stayed with them for three years before the call of farm life again became too strong, and they bought and moved onto a farm near Bellaire. It was there that their youngest child, Barbie, was born.

By this time their oldest boys were nearly grown and their older son Arnold Junior was inducted into the Armed Services. He spent two years in stateside duty and returned to find that the family had moved once more, this time to the farm they still occupy in Jordan Township.

That move was made in 1948 and only three children remained at home. The children were in Junior High, the same as my own children.

Soon the Harts and the Bundys became used to seeing each other's children banging in and out of doors and zooming by in some souped up jalopy. They always got along well together, and we enjoyed their company. But we were not prepared for the return of that soldier boy, who came home and walked right off with our oldest daughter Justine.

Nevertheless, that's how it happened—just as the story books say. We should have been warned.

Delbert is married now too and his boys work the farm he loved.

******

It was here that my original story ended but it was not the end of the story.

Arnold's children grew into adulthood, met their loves and left his home to make lives of their own.

Short handed now, Arnold turned his interest to a private well driving business. Becoming an expert at the job, he brought the blessing of running water to many of his own and adjoining communities. Then in his latter years he had the joy of working with and developing the skills of another first rate well-driver, his grandson, Richard Lundy son of his daughter, Theda, and her husband, Pete Lundy, who live nearby.

On the fifteenth of December Arnold attended the twenty fifth wedding anniversary celebration of Arnold Jr. and his wife Justine—my daughter. That day he had the same slow smile and the same glint of humor in his eyes that he had the first time I met him.

On the third of January he was taken with pneumonia, and on the twenty fourth of January after three weeks of intensive care in the hospital, and after a gallant fight, Arnold passed away. He leaves his wife Beatrice, five children and twenty eight grandchildren to mourn his loss.

And that is the end of the story—or is it? How can we measure the effect of a man's influence? In the years I knew him, Arnold has held out a helping hand to many people.

Will they not pass on his kindness? Perhaps there is never an end, but only a new beginning.

Anton Josifec, Czechoslovakian Pioneer

The time was 1870 and America had long ago won her independence along with the right to be known as a free people. The eyes of the eastern world had seen for themselves that the ability and sagacity of her statesmen was unparalleled, and the capability of her army and navy was only excelled by their courage and determination.

In Europe tales of the new world were on every tongue. As they talked of freedom, the demands of feudal life and the bonds of organized society seemed to chafe more than ever. So, to them, America became the symbol of escape.

From this atmosphere was born a growing pioneer spirit—especially from those countries where the people's first love was the land. Young men ready to strike out for themselves, young women of adventurous spirit, and often whole families filled boat after boat and headed for America, the utopia of the eighteenth century.

At least one country did what it could to insure the welfare if its people. Czechoslovakia sent advance agents to spot suitable locations and then published these findings in all the Czech papers.

This was an important service for the Bohemian speaking peoples, because community gatherings and church services played a large part in their lives, and without these activities they often became lonely and discouraged. For this reason, and because they did not speak English, it seemed advisable to find a good farming area where the people could settle in groups, forming their own communities.

We have no record now of the man who scouted this territory, but we know that someone traveled many miles of forests and streams, pushing through hills and valleys before they reached the local area known to us as the Bohemian Hills or simply "The Settlement."

Neither do we know how many may have settled here by following his directions. But we do know of one family who, oddly enough, read such a paper after they had already made the ocean voyage and settled in Racine, Wisconsin. This was the family of Anton Josifec.

Anton and his wife Antonettie came to America with five children—four girls and one boy. The youngest of the girls, Josephine, learned to walk during the trip.

For about two years the family lived in Racine Wisconsin, where Anton made his living as a bricklayer and stonemason, and during this time another child was born.

After reading an ad in their Czech paper that told of suitable land in Michigan, Anton and Antonettie decided to take advantage of the opportunity. And although they made the larger part of the journey by boat, they found that only a blazed trail led from the shores of the Jordan River.

At the end of the trail they found that the heavily wooded section was broken only by one small homestead, the Vrondicek homestead, which is today the Nemecek place. Anton and Antonettie boarded with the Vrondiceks until they could build a temporary home of their own on a fine central location in the section.

The Josifecs' first home was a log cabin that was roofed with green bark thatch. The cracks were chinked with moss and the slab door was sawed from a light basswood log. Only one small window brightened the cabin and home-dipped candles provided the only light on the long winter twilights.

Soon Anton and his neighbors built a railroad which made it possible to transport grain from Boyne Falls to Elmira to be ground.

At first all supplies were brought in from northern ports to landings at Advance or at the nearest other landing and bringing goods across the overland trail was very difficult.

But the pioneers rose to whatever challenge they met. One time Antonettie and two ladies from the Pesek family carried a full barrel of flour home from Rogers Bridge. The barrel, a reminder of the seemingly impossible feat still exists on their farm, a cherished souvenir of early days.

When conditions improved, the Josifecs built a new cabin a short distance from the first one and somewhat better, but their growing family now included nine children and the new home was soon outgrown too. Once more they built, relocating their buildings to accommodate the new place. This third house is still in existence and is as fine an example of the architecture of the time as you are likely to find.

In those early years there were many struggles but the Josifecs were lucky in that they understood the land. They worked hard and were careful husbandmen, and the soil produced. Often they were able to help later settlers and those who were less fortunate.

Soon the Josifecs were part of an actively growing community. They acquired the services of a Franciscan Father, Father Zorne, and services were begun in the front room of the Josifec's new home. Then before many years the residents of the Settlement built a church, where they often gathered in the evening to sit on the church steps and sing songs and tell tales of the old country.

In time Anton's daughters married and moved out of the house but his son, Tony, continued to live at home. He married Josephine Davis, who came over from their homeland to visit her sister. Tony and Josephine had two daughters, Jennie and Magdalene, and a son Ralph. They, along with other children, played around the church steps charmed by the music and fascinated with the tales.

Tony and his family built another house in 1906. In time his daughters married and moved away leaving their brother, Ralph, to take over the farm.

Ralph married Lillie Scuperwitz in 1942 and a third generation of Josifecs made their home in the Settlement. Lillie was a girl of his own nationality who came from Portage, Wisconsin. They still live happily in that last home with their ten year old daughter Lula.

With beautifully landscaped yards and pleasant homelike rooms inside, the Josifecs have a home and tradition to be proud of. Their only regret is the lack of a male heir to carry on those traditions.

As we credit the men of the family with handsome home-building, we must also credit the women with the beautiful plantings and landscaping. These are largely the work of Ralph's mother and his wife Lucille. One snowball bush is a family heirloom. Planted forty years ago by Ralph, it is a slip from a plant that his grandmother planted many years before. Both bushes reached a height of twenty feet.

Tony and Josephine as well as Anton and Antonettie were strong and sturdy stock. They all lived into their 80's and were able to see great changes in the Settlement and in the surrounding territory.

It is hard to write a finish to a story like this but we have the satisfaction of knowing that even if the family name should die out in the coming generation, the influence of the past and present generations will not be lost.

For their lives like the buildings they built, were strong and true. And those who knew and loved them feel that they have merely gone on ahead to do some more pioneering on another fairer shore.

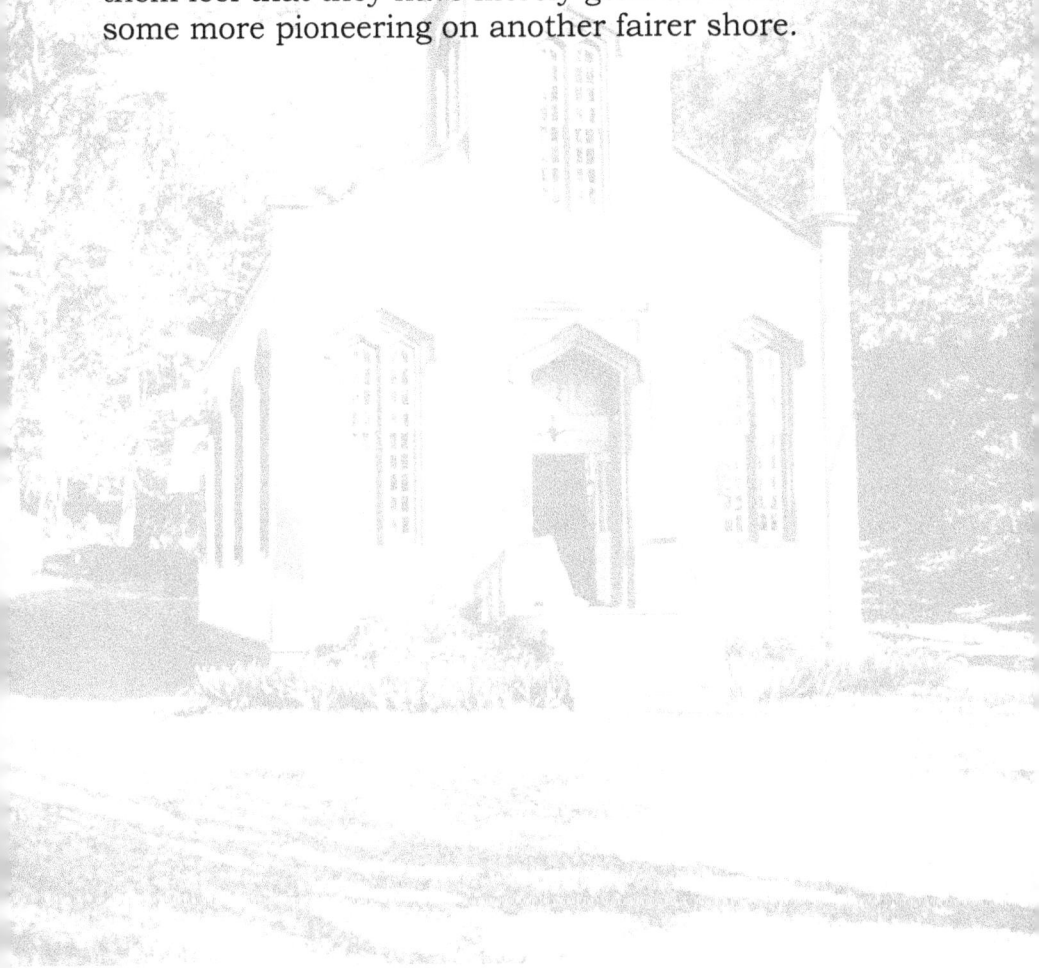

The Saga of the Craigs and the McLeans

This story begins in 1884, when Lauchlin McLean was at long last able to welcome his relatives to his home on the crossroads east of East Jordan. The family had traveled many long miles from Glasgow, Scotland and Lauchlin was happy to share the blessings of his new country.

East Jordan at that time was embroiled in a fight with Boyne City over the location of the county seat. East Jordan lost the battle the next summer, giving Boyne the honor which it held for thirteen years.

Although East Jordan was a lively little town with a fair population for that time, Antrim County, especially that part joining Charlevoix on the south, could still be considered new territory.

The first homesteaders, William Jaquay and his family, had settled in the county seventeen years before and a few others had followed, but new settlers in the valley region had to be pretty hardy souls to survive the rigors of claiming the land. There was still a good deal of big timber and the roads (so called) were more like cow trails, winding in and out among the trees. When someone driving oxen and wagon attempted the steeper hills, they had to contend with an impending possibility of a tongue over tailgate misadventure.

This then was the country as John Craig, lately a railroad office employee of Glasgow, and his family saw it when they arrived at the end of their journey. They had started months before and luck had been with them, for the long Atlantic crossing had been made in only eleven days. But when John, with his wife Catherine and their five sons, landed at Mt. Forrest Canada, winter was at hand and weather conditions were such that they decided to wait for spring before going farther.

But early spring found the family afloat again, for the trip was much faster and easier in those days if made by water. Sailing through the treacherous waters of the Great Lakes, the family came to the bay at Charlevoix. There they changed boats and took the inland route, arriving at last in East Jordan.

After a visit with Catherine's brother, Lauchlin McLean, the Craigs decided to settle on a piece of well situated land in the Jordan Valley. The land lay in Antrim County on the section line, with a small creek running through it and good rich soil.

Mr. Craig cleared a small section of the land and erected a log house, which was to shelter the family for several years. Those were not easy years for farming is never easy, and to support a family of seven on a farm that was mostly virgin timber kept them working from daylight to dark every day.

By the early 1900s John Craig had doubled his acreage through negotiation with a neighbor and now had sixty acres under cultivation. His farm was well stocked with sheep, cattle, hogs and horses. Horses were a specialty with him for horses were at a premium.

About this time John homesteaded another forty acre strip of swamp land and took logs from it to build a new and larger home.

The eldest son Jack also obtained lumber from the strip to build a home. Jack and his wife, Mabel Richards, whom he married in 1901, had purchased the adjacent farm on which to settle and raise a family.

Although these years were happy ones, some sorrow was mixed in for their second son Angus was fatally injured in a runaway accident. The young man was twenty three years of age and in the prime of life.

Then a few years later James, the fourth son, lost his life in a hunting accident. These were hard blows but somehow the Craigs held up with true Scottish perseverance.

After a long and full life Catherine Craig passed away in 1915. John followed only three years later, leaving three sons, Jack, Charlie and George.

Charlie and George stayed on the farm. They kept up the house and tended the fields until 1942, when Charlie passed away, leaving George alone.

Jack and Mabel, who remained on the farm they'd purchased years ago, raised a fine family of three boys and three girls. When their children were raised and nearly all married, they retired from the farm and moved into East Jordan. Here Jack enjoyed a few years of comparative leisure. He especially enjoyed getting together with other old timers for a few good yarns.

After Mabel's death in 1949 Jack lived with his children until he joined her in 1953.

There is now only the younger son George left to tell the tale of their first years in America. But he can tell you many things about the old roads, old farms and old neighbors. John Chatterton, Bill Webster, David Rainey and John Severance are all real people to him. And his stories include Mary Rogers and Frank Porter who were teachers of those times.

George finally sold the old home but it will still be known as the old "Craig Place" for many years.

Though tragedy found its mark in many of the Craig boys, the name will be perpetuated through Jack for many years. His eldest son, James, (deceased) who married Ruby Boyer (also deceased) had three boys as well as daughters.

Jack Junior, who married to Vernette Faust, also has a son and a daughter. And his daughter Elizabeth (Mrs. Clarence Morford) has children.

Gregory is now living in Saginaw with his wife Lucille Boyd. Ruby, who is now Mrs. Bud Cihak, is living in East Jordan as well as Flora who is widowed, and their brother Jack. They are well known as part of the economic and social structure of the town.

This was the way they came to be here. Yes, it started way back in 1884 with a spark of adventure in a Scottish heart and the raw courage to start over.

Hartungs: Romance and the Melting Pot
Part 1

This business of looking for beginnings is becoming more and more interesting. The trouble is, the further back one goes, the more interesting it becomes, and it is hard to find a stopping place. I believe the story I am starting this week is one of the best. It is not only interesting in itself, but makes us realize again the truth of the old saying, that "America is the melting pot of the nations."

It begins with four families who came to America, each from a different country. They were to join forces to become a part of the blood and bone of our country. It is the story of Maurice Hartung, American. It is the story of your neighbors.

First of all came Robert Burns from Ireland. He was a namesake and direct descendant of Robert Burns, the poet who has endeared himself to many generations. Our Robert Burns brought his family to the troubled zone of New York City during the hard years of the Civil War.

Robert was a sailor who had plied his trade on the ocean for several years before moving to Buffalo.

He began sailing the Great Lakes, but to one who had sailed the ocean, this was too confining. He soon retired to farm life because, "There isn't room enough to turn around."

Robert Burns settled on a farm in the Thumb area of Michigan, where his daughter, Margaret, met Henry Hazel. Henry had hired out to Mr. Burns to keep the crows out of his corn.

The boy, Henry, had quite a history for his people too had come a long way before they arrived in Michigan. It had been a long voyage crossing the ocean from England, but Great-great grandfather Hazel's courage was strong and it held the family together in the worst of times. After all, he had run away from home at the age of nine and had succeeded in making a living for himself ever since.

The trip was pretty hard on his wife and children, however, especially when the storm got so bad that the frightened crew was sure someone had committed a terrible crime. They thought someone should be hanged!!

Luckily they could come to no decision as to who it should be.

It was a happy day when the Hazel family disembarked after a six week voyage. They, like the Burns family, spent their first few years in Buffalo and were not far behind the Burns family in moving to Michigan. And as it happened, the Hazels settled as close neighbors to the Burns.

The lad, Henry Hazel, was glad to get his first job from Robert Burns at a penny a day, and I think he must have also spent many hours listening to the tales of the old seaman, for his life was to follow closely the pattern the older man had made.

Henry was only thirteen years old when he ran away from home. It was then that he learned to smoke and chew—habits that he gave up at the age of sixty.

But Henry did not forget Margaret Burns, for he returned later to marry her.

Still following in Mr. Burns footsteps Henry became a sailor on the Great Lakes. For thirty two years he was a sailor in summer and a lumber camp worker in winter. Henry followed the pattern to the end, finally moving to a farm in Sanilac County. The Hazels are still prominent farmers in Huron County.

But we will concern ourselves for the remainder of the story with their daughter, Sarah and her offspring.

Sarah married a boy by the name of Charles Srigley. Born of Holland and Elizabeth Srigley of Ontario, Charles was one of a family of six children.

Charles and Sarah named their first girl Hazel, and when their children numbered three, they bought 80 acres of cut over land bordering Carp Lake and moved to Levering.

It was a disappointment when the snow was gone, however, to find that their soil was mostly rocks, and after struggling with the land for seven years they gave up and moved to another place. They never guessed that that land would sell years later for $4000.00 as a resort property.

In time the Srigleys moved to Walkers Crossing, a sawmill town about three miles away, and when a young man named Eddie came peddling apples, young Hazel hid behind the door.

But you can not hide from fate, and Eddie and Hazel were yet to meet and marry. They were to become the parents of three children. Maurice the eldest of the children is the subject of this continuing story.

It was thus that the threads of the distaff side of his family were gathered. We have yet to hear his story and the story of his father. This will have to wait for another week.

Hartungs: Romance and the Melting Pot
Part 2

About the time that Sarah Hazel and Charles Srigley were settling down to raise their family, a young girl named Mary Jacobs left her home, a large medieval castle in Cardiff, Wales to follow her husband to America. In Wales the castle still stands—a monument to the years, but Mary's children to the third generation are Americans. Edmund and Mary Jacob-Williams established a homestead at Cecil Bay, Michigan.

Some years later a family named Hartung moved with their son, David, from Stratford, Ontario to work in the nearby Cecil Bay lumber camps and mills.

David and young Mary Jane Williams were attracted to each other and in time they were married. For a time they worked on a dairy farm in Ohio, but they returned to Michigan with their sixteen year old son, Eddie, the young man who sold apples and who so unnerved Hazel Srigley that she hid behind the door.

Like many young men of that time, Eddie was a lover of fine animals. He became an outstanding horseman who took great pride in his handling of the high strung driving horses.

One day in a deep snow plowed road Eddie saw three girls ahead of him. When he came near, they jumped to escape the high-flying hoofs of the horses and one of them slipped. Eddie faced a real test of his horsemanship to keep from running over the girl who would one day become his wife. It was Hazel, the girl who had hidden behind the door.

Not long after that Eddie was asked to take Hazel and a friend home from an outing. When faced with the question of who was to be taken home last, Eddie left the decision up to the horse. Hazel won and Eddie always says it was a horse who decided who would be the mother of his children. But I wonder a little if the horse didn't have just a little suggestion from the driver.

Ed and Hazel Hartung had three boys and two girls. They usually farmed in the spring and fall. Then during the winter they worked in the logging or pulpwood industry, and in the summer they worked on road jobs.

When the virgin timber disappeared, they moved to the Upper Peninsula, where they lived when their oldest son, Maurice, graduated from Grand Marias High School in 1931.

Maurice' father had passed away the year before and the family began to think of their old home at Levering. Then after three years they returned to the old place and spent the next ten years getting the farm back on a paying basis.

In December of 1944 Maurice made a trip to Flint to visit his sister. There a few days before Christmas he met a young widow, Eva Cannon-Rogers. Maurice was expected home on Thursday, but he didn't arrive until Monday morning!! He missed the bus.

Eva loved poetry and music and started writing at an early age. In 1942, while Eva's twin brother and three nephews were in the service, Eva wrote a good many patriotic songs. In fact she had made a promise to herself to write no other kind until her brother, Jim, came home. Of these songs there are several that received a good deal of recognition and publicity, even on a national scale.

Perhaps the best known of her songs was "The Blue Star Mother" which Captain G.H. Mains of Flint adopted as the official song of the National Blue Star Mothers organization. Second was "Onward Blue Star Mothers," which she wrote by request in honor of Adda Harris, first national President of the Blue Star Mothers organization. Still another was recognized favorably, "I'll Write You Every Day," a song dedicated to and used by Class 28 of the Army Air Force of Flint. During this time Eva also organized a Composers Club, in which she acted as President.

Soon after that Eva met Maurice and fate took a hand. The whole structure of both their lives changed. On February ten Eva and Maurice were married and moved to Levering along with Eva's three children from her former marriage.

They spent five years on the farm at Levering and then moved to East Jordan because they were "attracted by the fine people and by the excellent school system." In the 8 years since the move they have never been sorry for their choice.

Though the older children have married and gone from home, they still have a five year old girl whose name is Hazel Belle. She was named for her two grandmothers.

Eva is an avid gardener and she has made a beauty spot of her home. This hobby she mingles with song writing and photography. She is also a very talented colorist, doing work for photography shops from time to time.

Although this history has been quite long, I have really left out a great many interesting facts. I hope its many facets will justify its greater length.

The William Mohrman Story

To provide a little variety I am giving you a reprint of a little story I found in the Biographical History of Northern Michigan. It was written by one of Antrim County's pioneers, William Mohrman. It took place in Central Lake Township but it could easily have happened right here.

*****

When my folks and I moved here, Keefe's hill was right where it is now. The road, such as it was, followed the section line and he who came to the hill, finding he could not go under, around or through it, generally drove over it if his team could make it. But I have no doubt some intending settlers turned around and went back. I do not think John Keefe owned that exact spot called Keefe's hill. If he had, he would have disposed of it to someone on condition that the property be moved at once.

I have heard John hold forth on the beauties of this hill very eloquently and forcibly. Others too, with less eloquence and more force. We had a considerable sized trunk to bring in on wheels, and on gaining the top of the divide could look down into the intermediate valley and congratulate ourselves that the rest of the road would be easy—on the first trip only, for after that we knew better.

It was on that initial run that we had our first lesson in northland roads, and also our first lesson in corduroy. We followed a gulch that contained a series of spring holes, varied by stumps of all known varieties of hardwood. We had a good team and my brother drove.

In days to come, when I knew my brother would be late on the road, I would listen on still nights for them and could hear them as they passed over the top of the ridge. Then came a short period of quiet broken by a loud crash—ah the hemlock stump at the fifth mud-hole—shouts to the horses—now they are wallowing through the water-run—thump, bumpety-bump—they are on the crossway—now quiet—in the sand near the creek—a crash and a groan as the wagon lifts itself over the last obstacle safely—through once more.

I want to tell you about this stretch of road. In after years they improved it by changing it into a "hogsback" nearly as steep as a roof of a house. I had been out after deer with a good friend of mine who has been resting under the sod for many days. We had met the deer and fired at them, but they were not our deer. Finally we came out at this place tired, hungry and ugly.

I pointed to where the road had been changed to go up this impossible incline and asked, "What fool did that?"

"I did," my friend meekly replied. "They wanted it there. It makes no difference anyway, with both hind wheels locked and a stout neck-yoke they can slide down all right—and nobody will come here for a second time anyhow."

We had found temporary shelter in the unoccupied cabin of a settler and had before us the task of constructing a road to the homestead we had taken up on the east side of the lake. This meant the making of several miles of road, besides bridging the river. Our practice with axe and saw had been very limited, but our few neighbors gave what help they could at the bridge, and we finally landed at our claim and set about to build a house—of logs of course.

The road we had made was a perfect wonder of curves; we steered clear of all logs and brush heaps.

We had it made into a public road the following winter. When the road commissioner and surveyor came to establish it, the snow was deep and walking through the cedar swamps was very laborious.

In order to facilitate matters I laid a small flask on the corner stake and invited Cyrenius Powers, the surveyor, to take a sight through it along the line. This he did and said that while wine is a mocker and strong drink is raging, St Paul recommends small nips for the stomach's sake, and we all agreed that St. Paul was a scholar and ought to know. Evil minded gossips have since that time claimed that this was the cause of the crookedest road in the township, but they are wrong; the kinks were there before.

When we were getting the logs together to build the house, we were much bothered by wasps that stung our horses and caused them to run away, so we engaged a newcomer, who had brought a yoke of steers, to snake out the logs. Then one fine morning some time later the man turned up in our chopping with his animals and a travois, having wormed himself through the dense woods.

What psychological connection there is between profanity and driving oxen I do not know, but I am certain this man had graduated with high honors at some school where driving oxen is taught. I have heard of army mule drivers, who by a few "feeble remarks" could raise a blister on a mule's back, but this man was a champion.

Now it so happened that his outfit, with a twenty-six-foot log attached came near a large wasp colony that instantly swarmed out to see who knocked. They alighted on the driver and the steers. The driver ran up a small hillock and from there spoke his little piece to the oxen which floundered along, upset the log and smashed the travois.

When we had accumulated enough logs, we had a raising bee and about fifteen of our neighbors came to build the house, some as far as five miles. It was past ten in the morning before they got together, appointed corner-men and set the chips flying. Then arose the cry which no one hears nowadays: "Yo-heave! Up with the brouse end!" And they worked like Trojans rolling up the logs and fitting them together.

We had provided ample dinner and supper and they ate enough for forty men. At ten o'clock at night I announced the walls were high enough, though they declared they would put on another round if I gave the word, and the company broke up, going home through the woods in the dark. Some got lost and did not get home till the next day. And all this for strangers they had hardly ever seen."

*****

This story gives, a quite authentic picture of the early days of Antrim County. I hope you have enjoyed it.

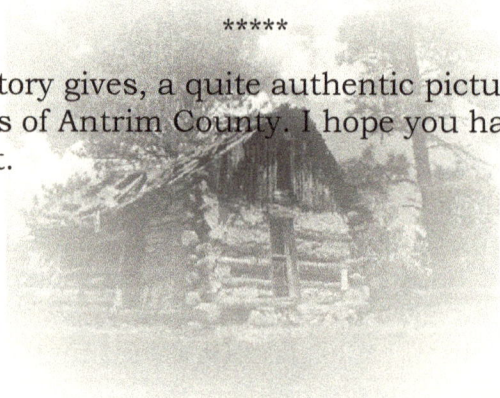

William Stevens: Veteran Pony Express Rider

Early Pioneer Homesteaded in 1855, Toted Grindstone from Elk Rapids on Back

This story is taken from a little different territory, it being a part of the history of Chestonia Township. I think, though, that many of you men and probably a few of the ladies who enjoy fishing, will remember casting your hook in the waters of a small stream located in Jordan Valley known as Stephens Creek. This story will give you a glimpse of it in early years and also make you acquainted with the one for whom it was named.

His name was William E. Stephens and he was born on Feb. 7, 1841 in New York State. The story of his boyhood has been lost in the shadows of forgetfulness, but we do know that he ran away to join Lincoln's soldiers at the tender age of seventeen.

Perhaps his youth was his best recommendation for the duties assigned to him in the next few years, for though he was attached to the 10'th Infantry Co. B, of New York State, he also, as a rider in the Pony

Express, became a link in the U.S. mail route between the east and the west.

Many of the definite dates and facts are lost or unauthenticated, but undoubtedly young William saw a good deal of real action during the time he spent in the service of his country. And during the rest of his life he liked nothing better than to spin the yarns of his many adventures. It only delighted him the more, when some of the more fantastic stories stretched someone's imagination to the point where they didn't know whether or not to believe them. Some of the tales he liked best to tell were of the meetings with President Lincoln and Brigham Young.

This colorful adventuresome life was cut short, however, when William was wounded and sent back to a New York hospital. He was shot through the hips and had a badly shattered leg as well as internal injuries sustained when he got an arrow in his side. He spent long weeks recovering with plenty of time to get acquainted with the nurses and to appreciate their tender and efficient care.

One nurse seemed to stand out above the others, and to her William lost his heart. They say that pity is akin to love, and I have no doubt that watching this young boy struggle through many painful hours brought about a tender place in the nurse's heart for William as well. At any rate, when William was finally able to leave the hospital Emma Wilcox, formerly of Virginia, was ready to go with him as his wife.

These times saw the beginning of an almost mass movement into northern Michigan. The Indian uprisings had finally been conquered and the wars were over. It was only natural that the young men who had done so nobly in battle should feel themselves equal to any hardship in the life of a homesteader.

William Stevens: Veteran Pony Express Rider

In 1856, two years before the first homesteader was to settle in Jordan Township, William and Emma decided to join the land rush and to homestead a place in Michigan. They faced a Herculean task for one whose health was and always would be somewhat sub-standard.

There was nothing sub-standard about their courage, however, and William, with his faithful wife at his side, settled in a small opening in the woods near a stream.

In only a few years there would be settlements in the area, and railroads that would not only bring in more people but would also make it easier to bring in needed supplies. But for William and Emma in those first years there were none of these conveniences and none of the pleasant things which follow when one has neighbors.

Needless to say goods were stretched as far as possible and settlers did without many conveniences, for all supplies at that time had to be brought in from as far as Elk Rapids. In William's case this had to be done on foot, but he did make the trip in those first few years whenever necessary.

It must have been an almost impossible trek, for William was partially disabled and walked with a cane, so the Stevens family did without many of the things we would consider necessary.

But there are some things a man feels he must have and one of those for William was a grindstone. For the big trees were hard enough to fell but with a dull axe it was impossible. After putting it off as long as possible a day came William knew it had to be done. He set out on foot for Elk Rapids.

There were a few homesteads between the town and their own home and the accepted method of travel was to go as far as possible each day and spend the night at some homesteader's cabin. Thus in several days it was possible to make the trips for supplies.

So William's first and last stops were made at their nearest neighbor, a man named John Call, who lived about four miles west of the present site of Mancelona.

After leaving the Calls on his return trip William arrived at the edge of the river, carrying the grindstone and some newspapers which he had bought, hoping to be able to catch up on the news. He looked for the log that was used to reach the other side, but the log was nowhere in sight.

Tired to the bone from the hard trip, William was in no mood to stumble around in the dark any longer looking for the log and the only way of getting a light seemed to be to light the newspapers, so this was what he did. Putting the grindstone down, he lit the papers, and holding them high, he walked up and down the bank until he found the log bridge. It worked too. The only trouble was that after he found the log and the newspapers were gone, the grindstone was no longer in sight so rather than lose the bridge again he decided to go on home and return the next day for the grindstone. And that is what he did.

As people kept moving north several settlements grew in nearby sites, and the creek became known as Stephens Creek. Then when the township was organized, the council decided to name it after William's and Emma's elder son, Chester, but when they searched the records, they found another township named Custer. So to avoid confusion they called it Chestonia.

As the area became more thickly settled and trains began to deliver mail regularly, a need was felt for a post-office in the town of Alba, and Mr. Stephens became the postmaster. He moved his family, which consisted by then of his wife and two sons, into town and began a season of comparative ease for William and Emma.

When Chester was only fifteen years old his mother, the faithful nurse who became a pioneer, passed away, leaving the one whom she had clung to through better and worse, very lonely indeed.

In 1888 William remarried a local girl, Mary E. Richard. William and Mary continued to live in Alba and three children were born to them, James, Emma and Bessie.

In 1897 William and Mary moved with their family to Mancelona, where they lived out the rest of their years on the meager pension of that time, which was only $25 per month. And on this they kept a family of five and even bought feed for a pony, a feat which would be impossible today.

William died in 1917 at the age of seventy six, but Mary continued to live on in Mancelona until 1950 when she too passed away.

In spite of the fact that Mr. Stephens had five children, there is only one living—his daughter whom he had named for his first wife.

Emma has been married to Archie Lueck since 1908 and they have two children. Next year they will celebrate their Golden Wedding anniversary. For thirty five years they lived on a farm near Mancelona, before moving to another farm near Bellaire where they remain.

During the time I spent with Mr. and Mrs. Lueck I was impressed by the quiet comfort and mutual affection that seemed to permeate the atmosphere.

The visible evidence of Emma's membership in the Garden club blends well with the collection of antique cups and saucers which she displays on several shelves in her home. Besides these hobbies she is also a member of an Extension Club and the Hospital Auxiliary.

Mr. and Mrs. Lueck are the kind of people it is a pleasure to know, and I would like to thank them for their interesting story with the little glimpse it gives us into the history of our county and into the lives of the people who opened the area to make room for all of us who follow.

Severance: Landmark Home

One of the residences in the area that I would place first in a list of "places of interest" is the old Severance home. It was once a part of an estate of fourteen hundred acres.

Sitting almost on the banks of the Jordan River and looking down on the road, it has been the home of a succession of respected and civic minded members of our community, of whom the present outstanding example is our Judge Severance of Bellaire. And we have no doubt the family will show more examples of the same timber in both this and future generations.

The old home was sold ten years ago and the place is no longer farmed, but the house is still there, looking down on the people of our community as they pass like an old friend. I remember a twenty mile buggy trip I took as a child with my grandfather. Of all the houses we passed this is the only one I remembered.

In my teens I visited the sugar house which sat among the maple trees between the road and the river. How interesting and m-m-m how good!

Mr. and Mrs. Bud Partee, present owners of the Severance farm, are giving the old house a "new look."

News

We haven't minded the winter so bad this year. It hasn't seemed so hard somehow. Then again we wonder if we are becoming one of the old-timers who always seem to say, "Winters aren't what they used to be." But one thing seems to get worse, the ice on the roads. You never know when you will meet yourself coming back on these county roads.

It does look as though improvement may be made on our Chestonia bridge location. Let's hope it happens soon.

Another thing that bothers me is the way small game is thinning out in this area. It seems to increase a little each summer, but it is very scarce again by spring. The only way I can account for it is the increase in fox and wildcats. Where are all those varmint hunters?

There is one residence that has looked pretty dead all winter. Mrs. Anna Kotovick has moved into East Jordan for the winter.

We hear that one of our neighbors, Ford Johnson, is getting out some logs from his swamp on Cedar River. Are you going to build or barter, Ford?

Anna Kotovich–Austria to America Alone

Fifty two years ago a young woman of twenty three came to America from her home in Austria. She spent eighteen years in New Jersey, Colorado and Detroit before she and her husband with their seven children came to Antrim County and built the farm she has lived on for the thirty four-years. It was in that home that Anna delivered her youngest son and raised her family. After her husband passed away in 1937 Anna carried on, never sparing herself or hesitating in time of need.

Three of Anna's sons (Terry, Johnny and Steve) as well as one daughter (Mary) have completed a tour of duty in the armed services and are doing well in civilian life.

Terry and Johnny are married and operate a guide service and bait shop in East Jordan. Steve stays with his mother and works in East Jordan. Mary lives in Detroit with her sister, Olga, and her family. Another sister, Helen, lives in Boyne City and a brother, Fred, lives in Traverse City.

Mrs. Kotovich always seems to be able to find nice things to do for others. And we are sorry to hear she has been ill for the past year. We wish her well.

Tidbits From the Mailbag

I have received mail from an old resident who has moved away and has sent me some interesting facts that I can use if I expand my horizons across the county.

I have at hand a letter from Mrs. Katherine Murdoch-Keen of Athena, Oregon, who lived in Alba and drove a team back and forth to Finkton—a town in Jordan Township that is nearly non-existent now—where she taught school.

It is a most interesting letter containing quite a few questions. Perhaps someone could tell her of the Ed Brown family or descendents.

She also says that a Mr. Dibble, a merchant of that time, spoke of a man who bought a grindstone in Mancelona and carried it to his home site in the Green River area. I would like to know who that man was, as my childhood home was also in that area.

Mrs. Keen tells me that in naming Star Township several suggestions were made, including "Hardscrabble" by A.J. Clark and "Freedom" by Fred Feller. But Edson Olds won when he suggested the name "Star."

There is more in the letter that I may use later when I have more space.

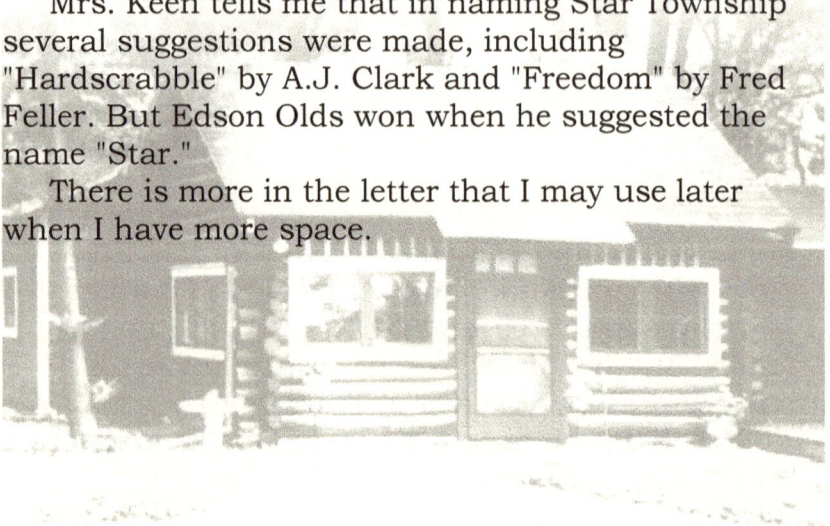

Trojanek

Mr. Dan Trojanek, son of Anna and Albert Trojanek, was born in East Jordan where he spent most of his younger years growing up with his 5 sisters on a farm in Wilson Township.

At age twenty he bought the farm and has lived on it ever since. Although he has tried working in the city, in woods and in sawmills, he always came back to the farm.

Shortly after Dan bought the farm he built his home and married a neighbor, Susan Jacobsheck. Of this marriage there was born one son, Dennis.

But the marriage was not to last. It was severed after a few years, and in October of 1954 Dan married his present wife, the former Mrs. Dorothy Farley. Oddly enough they both have the same birth date, July 10. Some of you may have seen them on the "Harry Entertains" program on their shared birthday.

Mr. Trojanek says the country has changed a great deal since he first moved into the township. One of the things he takes pride in is that he helped take off the last stand of virgin timber in section 27 of the county while working for the East Jordan Lumber Company in 1927.

Born in 1895, Mr. Trojanek is sixty one years old but his fields are always well cared for and his ambition never seems to lag. For several years he has not only farmed his own place but has done custom baling for his neighbors during the haying season.

News

Now that we are again able to cross the Chestonia Bridge, we are better able to admire and appreciate the improvement that has been made. Besides the better road it is now possible to go through the tile beneath the road with a boat. This should be of interest to all boating enthusiasts, whether their interest is centered in fishing or plain sight-seeing.

Mrs. Anna Kotovich was honored at a surprise birthday party Tuesday at the Vern Bundy home. Those present were Flora Pinney, Rena Morris, Minnie Gould, Bernice Johnson, Beatrice Hart, Flora Church, Anna Kotovich and her daughter Helen Coon of Boyne City. Ice cream and cake were served and Mrs. Kotovich received many beautiful gifts, including some from friends who were not able to attend.

A VACATION AFTERTHOUGHT

I set out to find on a hot summer's day
Relief from the heat and the every day grind.
The water was fine and with lots of sunshine;
And so I decided the week end to stay.

God knows I love beauty and the wonderful land;
He knows I need rest and He will understand!
So I swam and I played;
And I thought it was grand!

But later that night, when I turned out the light;
I looked up at the sky, oh so blue;
And I wondered if God would know where I was;
When He looked at my empty pew.

I looked up at the heavens and then swallowed hard.
I wished I was home in my own back yard.
Yes, I knew I'd done wrong and what was the worst
I'd turned my back on God and put myself first!

And what would I do when vacation was through?
When I needed Him badly, somehow;
Would He then be on vacation from me?
As I was from Him just now?

Can you imagine a god like that
Who would go on vacation and leave you flat?
No! My God of love is faithful and true;
And I want to be like Him in all that I do!

Yes, I know He'd be there where He said He'd be
In His house on the Sabbath, looking for me.
I had no more desire to wander and play;
I must be with my Lord on His special day.

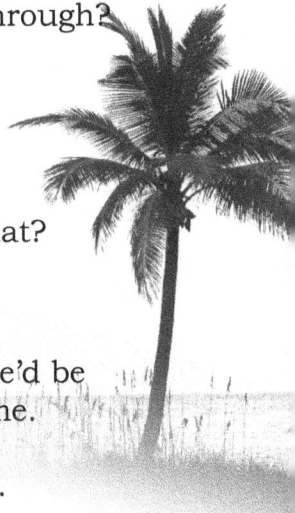

Birds and More Birds

Attention Sock Miller Bird Watching Friends!!

I think this week instead of introducing a person or place; I will present one of our feathered winter visitors. Although I have often admired the beauty of the Rose Breasted Grosbeak, he in no way outshines his yellow cousin, the Evening Grosbeak. I believe this is the first year I have seen the Evening Grosbeak.

In case you need help to identify him, let me give you a few pointers.

First, his size is eight inches—or slightly smaller than a robin, built chunky. He has a short blunt bill of bright yellow. The male is mostly a clear beautiful yellow with an olive brown throat and breast; and black wings and tail. The female is a duller shade; more or less suffused with yellow wings and tail blackish.

You can expect to see these birds almost anywhere there are seeds and buds to eat. They show little fear of people and are likely to land in a flock in your yard, if you have maple, elder, sumac or evergreens. If you have field glasses to study them, you have a rare treat in store.

It is recorded that in the year 1889-90 this beautiful bird descended in flocks on the New England and Atlantic states. However, they were killed in such numbers for their plumage that they never returned.

Winter visitors to the Mississippi valley and north western states, they spend their summers in Manitoba and northward.

At any rate, I'm sure if you get a glimpse of their brilliant yellows and blacks against the background of snow and see how easily they let you walk up to within a few yards of them while chattering and feeding, you will feel that you have found some new and lovable bird neighbors.

Here's hoping they get a welcome here that will encourage their future use of this route in their travels.

News

Road conditions here for the last few days have been such that to risk them at more than a minimum speed, one would have to be either ignorant or foolhardy. They are rutted and gouged at irregular intervals with evidence that makes even innocent victims suspect that they are being judged as one, the other or both.

Arthur Wycoffs

W hen rain drove me inside, out of my garden the other day, I decided to do a little visiting and news-gathering, and it wasn't long until I found myself on Highway 66 headed north.

I became attracted to a pleasant home site where I stopped for a visit with Mrs. Arthur Wycoff.

Born in Gaylord, Arline Wycoff moved to Detroit at an early age, but later returned to her birth home. While attending school in Gaylord, she met her husband who was working on a road job in Wolverine.

Arthur and Arline were married in 1935 in Burnips, where her husband was born and where he worked as a crane operator for Harry Pickett of Allegan. The couple stayed in Burnips for the winter and then followed the road jobs from place to place, wherever the work was available. Arline delivered their first son, Ralph, after two of their five years on the move.

Finally the Wycoffs moved to a farm near Martin, where their second son, Loren, was born. They stayed on the farm for 6 years, and in 1945 they bought a permanent home on the highway here in Jordan Township. The soil on the farm was good and the school was convenient. Mrs. Wycoff was happy to settle down. It was much better than traveling.

Mr. Wycoff's job left some time for working the farm, but as the boys grew older, they took over more of the farm work until they were almost handling the work by themselves.

They had one bad setback in 1951; their barn burned just after they had filled it with hay. Since then they have cut their stock to a minimum—two cows, a couple head of young stock, and one horse. There isn't room for more in the existing buildings and it has not seemed advisable to rebuild.

Ralph graduated this spring, and will start his schooling this fall at the Soo Branch of the Michigan College of Technology.

Loren at age fifteen belongs to Future Farmers of America and is looking forward to finishing high school, so he can enter college to study engineering.

As I came to the end of my afternoon, I thought to myself that it is too bad that more people can't have an excuse to stop and visit wherever they see a place that takes their interest. Of course one can always stop anyway but it is more difficult. For you who aren't able to visit at will, I write this column.

Gust and Mary Larson

Early Days Recalled by Mary Larson, Area Pioneer

You may think this a common story with little of special interest. And that is true. It is not what one would call sensational, and it is for this reason that it merits attention. It is the typical story of the home-loving men who built so well, spending a lifetime developing their homes and fields and doing their part in building their community.

On a quiet street of East Jordan conveniently located near the church of her choice lives a pleasant lady whose outlook is so young and cheerful, and her days so full of the activity that one seldom gets the impression of age, inability or loneliness. Nevertheless, Mary Larson is on intimate terms with all three.

In looking back on her eighty two summers she relives memories so different and methods now so outmoded that comparison is almost ridiculous. Mary was born in 1875 in the Green River Valley community of Antrim County, and even then Green River boasted a fair number of families. For such a pleasant stretch of land with plenty of water and good soil couldn't escape the eyes of men who came into Northern Michigan to work in the logging camps or to find places to settle down and make homes for their families.

In 1895 Mary married a young man whose surname was the same as hers. The young man, Gust, had recently arrived in this country with a group who had come over from Sweden. He and Mary moved onto a farm conveniently located near the river, the railroad and the country store.

The Post Office, run by Joe Miller, was one of the busiest places in the community. George Glassburn ran the blacksmith shop and Chancy Miller took over the first store. When the D&C Railroad went through, the station master was Ed Price.

Potatoes were usually a fair crop in the valley and there was a potato house to take care of them. The farmers filled the warehouse each year and a regular buyer came by from Petoskey to take them to market.

Gust was a thrifty farmer and a good dairyman, and in a day when a cow was seldom sold for poor production he always kept the best. There was always plenty of pasture since cows were commonly run on the cut over tracts of timber land.

When my parents moved into the community in 1916, it was through seeing them driving their cows through our yard every evening that we first became acquainted with the Larsons.

One day my father was helping me to learn the countries and their capitals for a school assignment. He told me I could remember the capital of Sweden if I thought of Mr. Larson bringing his "Stock home." It worked so well that I never forgot.

Gust and Mary spent forty four years on their farm and they kept boarders during most of that time. The rural school teachers nearly always stayed with the Larsons, enjoying the homey hospitality, the good food and the convenience of living relatively near the school.

Some of the more outstanding people who stayed with the Larsons were the Wards "Timber-Lookers" and the crew of "Square Timber" out of Saginaw.

One interesting man was a map maker. Day after day he took his men out to explore every hill, valley and stream. Each evening he returned to reproduce his findings on a section of paper which he fitted together with those sections which he had already finished.

In 1914, after Gust and Mary had nearly given up hope of a having a family, their son Karl was born, an added blessing in their busy lives. Karl grew up in the warm atmosphere of the Larson home and when he finished high school he decided to go to Michigan State College. Because of his love of the farm and his experience around his father's dairy herd, it was natural that he should choose to study agriculture and animal husbandry.

Very few young people from the farms would ever have considered college as a possibility for money was scarce in rural communities, but Karl's determination was as big as his ambition and soon he was off to the city. There he enrolled in college, found a job and settled down to the long job of working his way through school.

In 1943 while Karl was serving in the military, he received word that his father, who had been ill for a long time, had passed away. Soon afterward he was sent into the European conflict. There he saw a good deal of action as a tank commander including the Battle of the Bulge.

Alone now, Mary sold the farm and bought a home in East Jordan near relatives. Her home has a warm atmosphere that reflects the busy fingers of a real home maker, and her face still shows instant understanding and charity. It was this warmth that once caused her to be known by nearly a whole community as "Aunt Mary."

A Bear Goes to School on Stake-time

Mr. Staley was one of those who arrived in the area early on, but while others busied themselves with farming and logging, Mr. Staley became known far and near as an expert hunter and fisherman. He was one of the few who could locate a marauder and follow the animal until he brought it back. Often he returned from a hunting trip with a bear, deer or fox whose meat and hide he could use, sell or trade.

On one occasion Mr. Staley shot a bear and was bringing him home with his horse and buggy. As he passed the school, the children streamed out to the road to view the bear. The teacher, willing to please the children, had dismissed the entire student body.

At that time the school faced west instead of south as it does now and the only furnishings were a stove and several benches. A clock was considered a luxury in those days, but a stake had been planted in a strategic position in the school yard. When the teacher wanted to know if it was time to dismiss school, she went outside to study the angle of the stake's shadow. This method of telling time was known as stake-time.

New Neighbors: The Austins

I think I have some very interesting friends to introduce to you this week. Their names are Mr. and Mrs. Roger Austin. Although they are comparative newcomers, they have made a real place for themselves in the community.

Both Mr. and Mrs. Austin were born in Michigan. Their earlier years were spent in the southern part of the state, where they raised two children. Then in 1947 they moved to Jordan Township and a farm that was once part of the Severance homestead. The main asset of the farm at that time was twelve acres of cherry orchard, which was much in need of care. The house itself needed repair and that came soon after the Austins moved in.

The house was completely remodeled and modernized, and the Austins have added a beautiful study to their home. In it I saw a most impressive looking manuscript, which you may see in print someday.

The grounds were landscaped, the existing orchard was improved and more and more land was put into shape for trees.

Today the Austins have twelve acres of cherries, six hundred fifty pear trees two hundred plum trees and a one thousand-tree planting of apples of various varieties. These are expected to yield a high harvest this year. They also have several varieties of fruit in small numbers which are kept for private use.

Roger is interested in what makes the fruit look and taste good and has studied the secrets of the vegetable kingdom. Not only can he produce fruit of wonderful flavor but he can also tell you what gives it that extra flavor.

Mr. Austin is a member of the National Nut Growers Association and has planted several kinds of nuts in which he is very interested.

This couple would be a credit to any community and though they have already accomplished much, they are not the type to rest on their laurels. Their ambition and industry are boundless. If they were magicians, I would say, "I have a feeling they still have plenty of rabbits in their hats."

Meanwhile they are looking forward to a good year for their fruit farm. They believe this winter was an ideal one for the trees and everything points to a year of top production

A HANDFUL OF DREAMS

Once when I was young and life was new
I dreamed a dream;
Of great and valiant things that I would do;
Of daring feats and things impossible,
Or so they'd seem.

With all the words a jostling in my mind,
I could or really aught,
To do something really meaningful,
A sweeter song, a touching verse, a better book;
Or so I thought.

Soon days ran into years.
And somehow beauty, and the stuff of dreams,
Still coyly peep through crevices of duty.
I catch her now and then but can not hold her fast.
Just vagrant gleams.

Thomas Gould

The little train came chugging slowly into the depot. All day it had kept a steady pace through the storm. The windows grew more and more dark as the train progressed deeper into the wooded sections of land. Small towns became farther and farther apart.

It was with a great sense of relief that the crew finally urged the rugged little train with it's over heated engine into the Cadillac yards.

The passengers too, were glad to see the settlement. They were looking forward to a little exercise, a warm meal and a good night's rest.

Among the passengers was a family of three coming from Mason, Michigan to a homestead near the village of East Jordan.

The previous fall, in 1874, Thomas Gould had come ahead of his family to choose a homestead and file on it. Then he had picked out his building site and returned to take care of business details.

Now he returned to East Jordan with his wife, Alice, and their small son, Elmer. At that time Elmer was 6 years old and an only child.

After a night in the hotel, the Gould family woke to find that the storm still raged and the streets and yards were blocked with drifted snow. Nevertheless, the shrilling train whistle told them the train was to leave on schedule. So, carrying their luggage, the Goulds forged their way through the drifts while protecting little Elmer from the wintry blasts as much as possible. It seemed that the engineer was hoping to be able to ram through the drifts before they became packed and impassable.

The Goulds settled themselves in the coach and after much huffing and puffing, the little train started out. It made its way slowly, stopping many times to back up and take a run at the banks of snow and they progressed several miles.

When it became obvious that they were not going to get through, the engineer decided to return to Cadillac rather than run the risk of being completely blocked or running out of fuel, so again the Goulds found themselves descending the train steps with the other passengers. Again they found themselves making ready for a night in Cadillac.

In the morning there was more snow than ever, but the train whistle screamed its readiness and the passengers hurried to get their things and themselves through the drifts and seated in the coach.

And again the train returned to the station as it had the day before. It was in a most discouraged frame of mind that the passengers gathered at the station on the third morning.

But at last the sky was clear. When the train finally started they could sit back and watch the black smoke swirl past the windows. It formed fleeting pictures against the snow and they suddenly felt more cheerful.

Soon the little train began to pick up speed, and after some hard going, it finally pulled into the small town of Boyne City. There the Goulds must find other transportation for the last leg of their journey. Mr. Gould found an ox team and the family wrapped themselves well and started the long, cold but uneventful trip to their homestead.

Lodging the family with a near neighbor by the name of Pryor, Thomas Gould began the job of building a home. In spite of the virgin timber on his place, Thomas found it necessary to bring lumber all the way from Charlevoix.

In about two months their home was ready. It was complete to the cedar "shakes" with which they thatched the roof.

Thomas and Alice settled down with their son, Elmer, to a typical pioneer life.

There were not many neighbors in the area but the family found friends in the nearby Justice family. Mr. Justice was there to help Thomas with the building and his son, Johnny, became bosom buddies with Elmer. Later, however, the friendship came to a tragic end when Johnny drowned in Pine Lake while saving the life of another friend.

Although East Jordan was still mostly Indian camps, there was one white man, Sol Iseman. He had built a small building which doubled as home and trading post. Many of the necessities of the pioneers' life came by water from the trading post.

The Goulds traveled down the Jordan River and into the end of Lake Charlevoix. After making their purchases, they traveled back again by boat. This was much faster and easier method of transportation.

Thomas provided an income for his family by cutting fence posts and railroad ties. Here again the river proved to be a valuable asset. He floated the products directly from his farm to market in Charlevoix.

When Thomas found he needed a team of oxen to farm the fields, he made a deal with his brother-in-law, James Richer. Thomas bought one ox and his brother-in-law bought another. These they traded back and forth. It was quite a satisfactory arrangement.

The Goulds received mail about twice a month, when a rider went through from Alba to East Jordan. The mail was a much looked forward to event. But one day a strange letter came with a black border. The letter bore news of Alice's mother's death.

For seven hard years the Goulds had stayed on their homestead and they liked it more and more as it developed, but Thomas and Alice returned to southern Michigan to care for Thomas' father. They stayed with him seven years and their second child, Flora (who became Mrs. Allison Pinney) was born.

By that time Elmer was a teenager and not at all pleased to share his parents. He tried to ignore Flora and this brought great pain to her, but as with all boys of that era, he soon began working away from home.

And so it happened that Flora was almost a young lady before the two siblings really got to know one another, and Elmer learned to care a great deal for his sister. "I knew men fell in love with the girls they marry," said Elmer. "But I had to fall in love with my sister." And so the estrangement ended happily in an unusually close brother and sister relationship.

In time Elmer married Mable Beebee and moved to Ohio where they raised three boys.

Finally the Goulds returned to the Jordan Valley, bringing with them a fine team of well behaved horses and two brothers-in-law to help build a new house. But luck was not with them for one day, while the usually well behaved team was drinking in the creek, a mysterious explosive sound filled the air. The Goulds later learned that The Red Mill in East Jordan had blown up, sending the sound thundering up the Jordan River to the farm. The horses were so frightened they ran away.

One day the woods near their place caught fire. Thomas tried in vain to put the fire out with barrels of water which were hauled from the creek. When he realized he needed help, he rang the dinner bell desperately and neighbors came from all around to help—some from clear across the river.

Although she was still quite small, Flora was put in the hay mow with pails of water and a dipper. She was to douse each spark as soon as she saw it. She spent the entire afternoon in the stifling barn and did her job so well that although the fire burned over many acres and many sparks had to be drowned, the barn and the winter's supply of hay was saved.

With Elmer away from home, Flora was the obvious one to help with the numerous outdoor chores. She learned to handle horses and many times she worked side by side with her father.

In spite of being her father's right hand man, Flora's education was not neglected. When she was five years old she started school in the log building that still stands near the foot of Mt. Bliss. The new school, which was built later for the district has been reduced to rubble for many years.

One of Flora's most pleasant memories of school is a day when the First Day Picnic was rained out. Seeing her disappointment, her father came to the rescue. He made the rounds inviting all to come to his house. Later in the day the rain cleared up and games and races took place as planned. That made it a perfect day.

A not so pleasant memory brings forth visions of a cyclone that went through. It cut through a great swath of trees, leaving a deep impression on the school children.

Flora took her ninth and tenth grades in the new school. Howard Severance was the teacher and he was very good to the children. They were all fond of him and felt much sorrow when he lost his life in an electrical storm the next summer.

In 1904, a year after her graduation, Flora married a teacher named Allison Pinney.

In time Flora's mother became ill and she came home to care for her. In 1914 while she was with her mother Flora's first child, Gould Junior, was born. In 1916 Alice passed away of a malignant illness.

In 1917 Thomas remarried and had two good years before he took a fatal illness.

Thomas' second wife, still known to many as Auntie Gould, spent many happy years with Flora and Allison. Still beloved by many she passed away in 1957 and was taken home to the Upper Peninsula to be buried.

Only a few months later Elmer and his wife, the former Mable Bebee, passed away within a day or so of each other. They were laid away in a double ceremony.

Meanwhile Earl had married a neighbor girl by the name of Minnie Crawford in 1910 and built a home nearby. In 1940 he had a severe case of appendicitis and passed away leaving his wife and two children.

These are the kind of people who make our country strong.

Andrew Huerta

A story doesn't need to be of olden days and primitive living to be interesting, and I feel quite sure that many of you would appreciate some stories of our younger and more recently arrived.

The Jordan Township locals have mentioned from time to time the names of Andrew and Emily Huerta, and as they are comparatively new residents, I hope you will be interested in a brief biography.

Andrew and Emily were both of like nationality and both from good sized families—Andrew, one of nine and Emily the second child in a family of five.

Andrew spent his early years in his birth town of Chicago. Then his family tried farming for a few years but a great flood occurred and his father contracted arthritis while wading in water to his waist trying to save his crop of corn.

Returning to Chicago, his father ran a tannery but he became more crippled as time went on and finally was unable to work. When his condition became tubercular, he retired to Fennville, Michigan where he lived with friends until his death.

In order to support her family, Andrew's mother started a confection and stationery shop. Andrew was then in his teens.

Emily also was born in Chicago and spent all her younger years there. At the age of seven she too lost her father, and although Emily and Andrew spent most of their youth living within a block of each other on the same street, they were grown before they met.

Once they met, however, their friendship grew rapidly. In 1943, faced with opposition to their relationship, the couple eloped to Minneapolis.

Returning to Chicago, they bought a home where they spent the next seven years working in the factories weekdays and pursuing other activities on weekends. They liked to fish on Lake Michigan or make trips to Fennville to see old friends and visit the cemetery where Andrew's father was buried. After each trip, they became less satisfied with their home in Chicago.

So they purchased twenty acres of land near Fennville. But work in Fennville was scarce and after six months of driving twelve miles to work at a low paying job, they moved to Grand Rapids, where they both found good jobs. Once more able to enjoy their weekends in the old way, they ventured farther and farther north.

Returning from one of these trips in 1953, they became lost. While driving back and forth looking for M-32, they found themselves on old 66. There, in passing, they noticed a nice looking farm with a FOR SALE sign on it. After driving aimlessly around the county for some time, they finally found 32 and followed it to East Jordan. There they stopped and phoned the real estate agent to make arrangements to look at the place that same day.

To look was to be charmed and Andrew and Emily emptied their pockets of all change left over from their weekend vacation to bind the bargain. Then they took off on a flying trip to Traverse City to make arrangements for the down payment.

The next year passed slowly but by the end of the year they were ready to move onto the farm with a clean slate. So in 1953 there were new neighbors on the Frank Atkinson place, and it was soon obvious that they would be not only neighbors but good friends.

Andrew and Emily both work, and Emily spends long hours at her hobby of baking. Her cakes are a work of art. Mr. Huerta's special interest is guns and sporting equipment.

The Huertas keep a very pleasant home where a visitor is always welcome. This is the family as you will find it any day—not pretentious but friendly and likeable people, who did a good deal of looking and then had to get lost before they could find the home of their dreams.

Recently, when plans for the new super highway through Chicago were revealed, it was found that it would be going right through both of their old homes. Emily's step father settled the problem very well, however, by building a new home in Junction City. He is a cabinet maker by trade and he did the work all himself, in spite of the fact that he is 76 years old.

John Murdoch: The Lure of Adventure

Early settler in Alba Area, Helped Build Congregational Church in 1883

This story has its beginnings in New York State from whence a good many of our early Michigan pioneers came. Although New York was still growing and opportunities were many, the hardy youth of the age abounded in the spirit of conquerors. The lure of adventure which seemed to beckon from the unsettled lands was an insidious thing. It always promised more adventure and greater opportunity just a little beyond their known horizons.

The immediate scene is that of a small town called Cazanovia. It was an early town of Dutch tradition, and its neat streets and well kept homes had already developed an expanding resort trade. It had beauty and permanence. Why should one ask more?

Yet many adventurous young souls used the town merely as a jumping off place on their way to other areas, where they seemed to see a gleam of the pot of gold at the end of the rainbow.

Among the residents of the town was the Murdoch family. Descended from really early American stock, the children could claim eligibility to the Sons and Daughters of the American Revolution organization—through their mother at least.

But as their son, John came of age, he looked long and often toward the west, and in his heart he set his face in that direction with no turning back.

Michigan was as yet new territory and although not too far from New York by today's standards, it was a long way into the wilderness for young John Murdoch.

In 1878, at the age of thirty one, John married Mattie Raymond who was born and raised in Galesburg, Michigan. Then four years later he and Mattie decided to take advantage of the low priced land available through the Agricultural College Grants, and in 1882 they chose a home site in Star Township of Antrim County.

Of course, at the time Antrim County was just another bit of dense forest; and there were no markets, no place to take the logs and no roads on which to deliver them. Still the timber had to be gotten out of the way, so it was cut and that which could not be used for firewood was piled in great heaps and burned. These great pyres lit up the country for miles around and destroyed thousands of dollars worth of lumber by present day prices.

There wasn't much glamour to the lives of those early pioneers. It is distance that gives it that appearance today because we see now the growth and development they accomplished. It was agonizing labor for them and growth was so slow it seemed almost imperceptible. They endured the sub zero temperatures in winter and the scorching heat of summer. Yet it was in their generation that the great miracle of change was brought about.

Then men and women came behind them moving up the rivers and lakes, settling in villages and spreading out into the forests. Each had a part in the development of the country.

Some who came were unable to stand the strain of work and weather, and after a few seasons they moved on to fairer fields. But where they had been, they left a rude cabin, a cleared field or a small orchard to provide a better foothold for those who inevitably followed.

But John Murdoch was not one of those who gave up. Even though the next few years while their children were growing were hard ones, he had a good help mate in Mattie and together they stood their ground.

In those days everyone took a keen interest in their neighbors; perhaps they realized that without each other their chances of survival were much smaller. So it was that in times of emergency or disaster the people gathered together to work toward one another's success. And many were the work bees, barn raisings and quilting parties that were enjoyed by all.

The year after John arrived in Antrim county a group of neighbors, including John, got together to build the Congregational Church of Alba. John Murdoch also worked with Mr. Starks to clear several plots of land for incoming settlers.

About this time the lumber companies began to spring up and the Handle Factory moved into Alba. These were a boon to many settlers because they provided a means to dispose of the timber as well as bringing additional income.

These are the years remembered best by John and Mattie's children, Katherine, Archie and Bertha. They were years when their father had no horse but worked hard enough to make up for it—years when he walked the five miles to town for groceries or other necessities. On these occasions the children waited anxiously because they knew there would be a stick of peppermint candy for them as a reward for being good.

It was only three fourths of a mile to the District No. 3 School, and it was especially pleasant for the children to wander along the woodland road in spring after the winter's cold and drifts. They learned the places to look for each woodland treasure—mushrooms in the spring or berries in the summer, or perhaps a bouquet of the beautiful wild flowers that were so abundant to take home to mother or to grace the teachers desk.

Katherine loved the woods and wild life and she treasures the memories. She tells of a deer she came upon unexpectedly and of a mother partridge that flew angrily toward her face as her little ones scampered into hiding. She also tells of a time when she walked to school in a windstorm and a big maple tree was suddenly uprooted and fell in the road a few feet ahead of her.

There was always plenty to do on the farm for parents and children alike. All pitched in, whether gathering berries in the summer or gathering sap for boiling in the spring. Often John made from fifteen to twenty gallons of maple syrup, and when you figure anywhere from one to two barrels of sap for each gallon, you begin to see the labor involved. It takes a long time to gather and boil down a barrel of sap!!

But all this hard work had broken down John's health and in February 1, 1899, nearly seventeen years after his arrival in Antrim county, John Murdoch passed away and Mattie survived him only until the following July.

The children were separated then. Relatives took the two younger children and Katherine went to Ferris Institute in Big Rapids. She secured a teacher's certificate, and taught second grade for a number of years. During that time she went to Ypsilanti for the two year teaching course and later took a job teaching in Oregon. While there she married and in 1913 she went to live on a wheat ranch.

Archie later joined Katherine in Oregon where he passed away in 1921.

Bertha followed in Katherine's footsteps and after teaching for two years in Michigan, she also moved west. In 1920 she married and at present she lives in the state of Washington.

Thus goes the story of a real pioneer—a story that parallels the history of our country. For three generations the story travels across the nation from New York to Washington. Who knows what the next three generations will see?

If they pursue their careers with the earnestness and integrity that John and Mattie Murdoch showed, they will leave a record to be proud of.

William and Minnie Kupp

To introduce you to this week's subject I will take you back to the late 1890's. At that time a great deal of Jordan Township was still in timber. Detroit was just beginning to produce the first cars and it was then that a Detroit couple by the name of William and Minnie Kupp became the proud parents of a boy they called William.

Young William grew with that city and in the next decade many changes came about in little William and also in the city. As the city was gaining width and breadth, William grew in knowledge and stature.

In attaining mature status, Detroit espoused itself to the automobile industry that was born in the city. Likewise, William grew in maturity and became espoused to a native Detroit girl named Lavina Lotz.

The years that followed were full ones for the Kupps. Lavina made a home for her husband and the two sons that were born to them, and William served a full thirty years as a School Engineer.

The wear and tear of city life began to tell on William though, for during the later years of their residence in Detroit Mr. Kupp's health began to fail. So at every opportunity they availed themselves of a friend's invitation to vacation at their place on Deer Lake.

Besides enjoying these vacations thoroughly, it was always a pleasant surprise to them to see how much William's health improved after a few days or weeks spent in the north. This finally convinced them that they should settle here permanently.

The home they bought in 1950 was unfinished, but that only provided something to do on weekends and vacations. It made them more anxious than ever to settle in their new home, and they finally made the move on December 31 of 1954. This was the beginning of a new kind of life for them.

Born and raised in the city, though they were, they adjusted like "ducks to water." They are very happy in their new home where Mr. Kupp indulges his hobby of carpentry and Mrs. Kupp likes to work outside in her garden or lawn.

Robert Kupp, the older son is now twenty four years old and is married to Mary Ellen Darling of Detroit. The couple has two daughters.

A chemical engineer, Robert spent time in the Armed Service at the Atomic Plant of Oak Ridge Tennessee. Since his discharge, he has become employed by a private business firm engaged in Nuclear Physics.

Though Robert's home is in New Jersey, his business requires that he commute to New York, Boston and other points. At present he is en route to Italy. While there he will visit Rome, Milan and other places which are to most of us merely another point on the map.

The younger son, William, is as yet unattached and has returned to Detroit. There he is serving an apprenticeship as a pattern maker.

Mr. Kupp's health, although improved, keeps him close to home and Mrs. Kupp is seldom seen far away. But when the opportunity arises to visit with her, we find a fine person with a friendly manner who is deeply devoted to her family.

We were proud to welcome these native Detroiters to our community and hope they will continue to be happy here for a long time.

The Wildfongs: Two Men Named Sam

Wildfong Family Among First Settlers in Mancelona; Came from Canada in 1875

This is the story of two men named Sam. I'm sure most of you know the one who tells the story, but many of his memories are of another Sam of long ago. Perhaps a few of you knew him too.

The first thing that Sam Wildfong can remember is the heaving of a small boat. His father was handling the oars, but making slow progress against the great broken chunks of ice which kept crashing into the sides of the boat and often blocking the way. Often the blocks were so big that a new course had to be set but each time the boat would veer to the south again.

The stern determined expression on his father's face erased any thoughts of turning back. Although his brother, Levi, and older sister, Mary, sat in the center of the boat with him and watched over him, he would much rather have been with his mother in the bow. But the haven where he longed to be was filled by his new baby sister Louise.

It was the year of 1875 and Sam was 2-1/2 years old. His father, Sam Sr. was a farmer from Stratford, Canada. Ever looking for opportunities to better himself, Sam had determined that the United States should be his new home. Once he had decided, he delayed no longer than necessary.

So, early in February of 1875, when the ice was just beginning to break up, he took his family in a small boat and braved the dangers of the weather. He depended only on his quick eyes and strong arms to get the family past the drifting ice floes and deep waters and into a safe port as quickly as possible.

And God must have been with them, for the tiny boat, which was only a speck on the great lake, made a safe passage and so brought the root and branch of a new vine to be planted in the new country.

The rest of the trip was made by train and when Sam Wildfong Sr. and his family arrived in Mancelona, they were met at the station by John Grody with his mule and cutter. They were taken to a little cabin near what is now U.S. 131 and M 66 corners. There they were to spend their first year, while Sam looked around for an available farm suitable for his needs.

He finally made a deal for a farm in the Green River Valley that was known as the Willard Harris homestead. It suited his needs better than most because it already had a house and barn. The story is told that Mr. Harris was a big man, and because he had no mule, he cut the logs and carried them one by one on his shoulder to build the house and barn.

Mr. Wildfong acquired a team, so when he moved his family onto the farm a year after their arrival, he had a yoke of oxen, a twenty five pound sack of flour and fifty cents in his pocket.

At first there was nothing to do but burn the logs. Only later were the Wildfongs able to sell bolts to the Wetzell Handle Factory. They hauled many loads by ox team to Wetzell, receiving the magnificent sum of $1.75 a cord for each load.

It was while working in the logs a few years after they came to the farm that a strange thing happened.

Mrs. Wildfong and Levi were working at loading the logs and Levi, who was then 9 years old, was holding the handspike. The oxen tipped over the sleigh and a huge log rolled off the sleigh and onto Levi. Fearing a fatal accident, Mr. Wildfong grabbed the log and lifted it off the boy.

Later, when Levi was proven to be all right, Sam found that though he tried with might and main, he was unable to do so much as budge the log.

Sam Jr. started school in an old log building that sat on a part of the farm now known as the Marshall Douglas place. He attended two years before the new school was built.

He studied under Miss Maud Plummer, who later became the wife of the well known Sheriff Bill Kittle. Years later Mrs. Kittle came to Sam's aid when he needed to get his naturalization papers.

Meanwhile Mr. Wildfong had cleared thirty five acres of land and raised potatoes and grain as well as cattle. Nevertheless, he found that with his growing family he needed to cut every corner possible to meet expenses. So he took a job as postmaster, a county office which has been obsolete for many years. He served in a sub-office of the Road Commissioner, which made it possible for one to do road work in lieu of payment of the now non-existent Poll Tax. Mr. Wildfong held this office for several years under John Rifenburg, who was then Road Commissioner. Today the Road Commissioner's office has been omitted.

For thirty three years Sam and Christina worked the farm while their family was growing up, but the strain of the hard life had been too much for Sam's heart and in 1908 he passed away.

So the story of one man named Sam came to a close and that of Christina narrowed down to a few more years. She did a fine job of holding the family together with some help from her second husband, Milton Kyke, whom she married after a period of eight years.

Christina was a large woman whose features so shone with good nature and love of her fellowmen that you saw only the sweetness of her character. Always a home lover, she could nearly always be found neatly aproned in her home or garden.

Any young mother could get helpful advice from her. And no one was ever turned away from her door hungry or tired. It is easily understood why she was loved by everyone and although she lived at Mayfield for the last few years of her life, those who had known her were deeply sorry when she passed away in 1936.

Sam Jr., who was in his thirties when his father passed away, began to think of a home and a place of his own. He looked around and finally bought one not far from his parent's farm with an old frame house that stood on a hill like the city of Rome. Located a little farther north, there was only the rural cemetery between his farm and the Douglas farm.

Sam met and married a young school teacher in 1918 and moved at once on to the farm where the Wildfongs lived for two years.

On the 6'th of March in 1915, according to the custom of that time, Sam held a barn raising bee and the greater part of his new barn was put up in a day. In that same year Sam built the new stone house which has become a landmark and can be seen for miles around.

For thirty nine years Sam and Alma were a solid part of the community. They lived their whole married life in one place, making many improvements and bearing eight children. And they still found time to be interested in all civic or neighborhood affairs. Having a fundamental belief in spiritual things, they also took a leading role in the Sunday school, where they carried the major part for many years.

In 1917 Sam and Alma had a well stocked farm and good buildings. They were well thought of in the community and had six living children. One child, whom they called Joe, was yet to be born and one infant daughter had died several years before. These children were Walter, Orlo, Dorothy, Edith, Harold, Bob and the baby Juanita.

Walter the oldest died at fourteen years of age after only three short days of illness. He was his mother's pride and joy and she never fully recovered.

Although she was a hard worker, Alma had a great deal of sickness in her last years. In 1952 she succumbed to a heart ailment, leaving a legacy of cheerfulness and many memories for Sam and her seven living children.

By this time most of the children were married and all were gone from the farm. With Alma gone Sam had little incentive to stay on the farm and he sold it the next year and moved to town where he could be near his sister, Lou, whom we all know as Lou Doerr.

His son, Orlo, established a garage business in which he and his brothers worked. At this date Orlo, Harold and Bob are still living in Mancelona with their families. The other children, all married now with families of their own, have settled in various cities of several states.

Sam himself remarried in January of 1954 and lives quietly with his wife, the former Alta McClish, within calling distance of some of his children and his sister Lou. He is quite proud to be able to tell you that he has twenty three great grandchildren and he really enjoys telling about those early days— even as far back as the small boat fighting its way across the ice choked channel.

Through the Eyes of Mail Carrier, Archie Howe
Part 1

I am stepping into Charlevoix County to pick up my subject for this week.

Although Archie Howe is not actually a resident of our township, he has had a definite part in the daily life of this district for many years. For thirty five years he has had the opportunity of observing and taking part in a good many of the trends of our changing times.

In 1924, when, for reasons of his health, Mr. Howe and family moved from their farm home into East Jordan, he took over rural route No. 5. This route had only been established since 1907 and in those fourteen years it had already changed carriers four times. Walter Davis had covered the route for the three preceding years, and when he was transferred to the post office, Mr. Howe was hired to fill his place.

Route 5 in 1921 consisted of twelve and one half miles of road which was remarkable only for its degree of "badness." The road went up hill and down with U turns and switch backs and gravel and deep sand. Of course there were occasional stretches of swampy land and the road there bumped along over a corduroy bottom.

Arche's faithful team, Dick and Bud, were more friends than servants to Mr. Howe, especially in the winter, when storms and bad weather often kept him on the road from before daylight to 4 P.M.

There was one especially bad time that left a clear cut memory for Archie and that was the bad storm that hit on February 21, 1922.

It caught him at Charlevoix and he had some difficulty getting back home. It didn't matter though as far as mail was concerned, for no train got through for ten days. When it did get through the mail piled up in an avalanche. For twenty four hours the post office staff was shut in, sorting and organizing the outgoing mail. Even that did not finish the job for they did not put the final pile of sorted mail aside until two weeks later. On the first day of April, one month and ten days later the D&C train finally got through.

I remember one such wait in 1918—a crucial time in the war arena for our soldiers over there. I have very clear memories of my father walking the floor trying to imagine what was happening. How much a radio would have meant to us then!!

Other things I remember concern the breaking up of the heavy ice crusted roads. All the men in the neighborhood got together and—using discs, drags and rollers pulled by teams that frothed at the mouth—they waded belly deep through ice crusted snow. As they worked, the ice and snow fell to one side stained pink with blood where the ice had cut their legs when they broke through the surface.

With this experience in mind, I can picture the difficulty Mr. Howe faced when, with his sleigh loaded to capacity, he started out with Dick and Bud to cover his route of twenty five miles of country roads.

The days of horse drawn mail delivery were not all hardships though. There were many times when the leisurely trip along the country roads was a pleasure. For one who was raised on a farm, each season had a special meaning and each crop that adjoined the road was noted.

There were even some amusing incidents that linger with the more serious ones. Like the event that occurred one day up in the Vance district. Mr. Vance's dairy bull got loose and was standing in the middle of the road disputing the right of way. The horses became spooked and Mr. Howe had all he could do to hold them.

Mr. Vance's dog saved the day, however. The dog burst forth and chased the angry bull back in where he belonged.

Such incidents are certainly amusing in retrospect, but one cannot be sure if they would be amusing or tragic at the time.

There are several people that have a special place in Archie's memories of those old days. One of them was Tom Bartholomew. He often invited Archie in for hot coffee and some lunch and to get warm by the fire.

Another friend in need was John Carney. Mr. Carney was situated on a very bad piece of road. And he often got out early and cleared the roads for Mr. Howe. These friends in need were friends indeed!

This then is what carrying the mail was like during the first ten years of Archie's service here. There are still many interesting things to be told. I hope you will read about them next week.

Through the Eyes of Mail Carrier, Archie Howe
Part 2

I n 1930 the Snowmobile was given a lot of publicity and quite a few rural mail carriers, who had spent hours during the day watching their teams fighting their way through the drifts, decided they were at least worth a try.

They were too!! It certainly was a relief not to have to struggle with the icy harnesses early every morning. And the saving in the amount of time required to cover the winter roads along with the extra comfort they provided was wonderful.

Mr. Howe really enjoyed his snowmobile and drove it for three winters from 1930 to 32. There was one objection though and that was the expense. All that ease of travel could not be accomplished, even by a snowmobile, without putting a lot into it. A snowmobile needs a lot of care. The treads need to be inspected carefully daily, and they need gas—and more gas.

After three winters Archie gave up his snowmobile and purchased a Model A Ford. The day of horse drawn deliveries were over!!

Many strange things rode with Mr. Howe on his mail route during his thirty five years of service. Part of his route was quite hard to get in and out of during the winter months and he often obliged the patrons by doing errands for them. Sometimes he stopped long enough to give someone a hand at some odd job. Twice he helped owners to get one of their cows out of a ditch. Once he took time to climb to the top of a windmill and do a repair job.

There was a day, too, when he came along just in time to help two men whose car had rolled over and pinned them both beneath it. That time he took time to rush them both to a doctor.

Most days though were without incident. Archie went the whole route observing the changing of the seasons and the movements of the wildlife. In all those years Archie never saw a lynx. He never saw a bear or deer until fifteen or twenty years ago. In spite of the stories to the contrary, there was little that could be called big game in the lumbering era of Jordan Township.

Mr. Howe has had very little trouble over the years and no serious accidents. The only accident that could have been called serious was so funny he still gets a laugh out of it. It seems he ran into the river by the Chestonia Bridge, and while his car was standing upright on its nose in the water, he watched one tire and his hat go floating down the river side by side. Then he climbed straight up over the back end of the car and jumped to dry land without even getting a foot wet.

There have been a lot of changes since Mr. Howe started. Now known as Route one, the route no longer takes in the Vance district and although his mileage has increased from twenty five and one half miles to fifty five and one half miles, the improved roads and methods of transportation have cut his time on the route down to four hours. In other words he has doubled his distance and cut his time on the route to half.

Mr. and Mrs. Howe live quietly in their comfortable home in East Jordan where Mrs. Howe takes part in community activities and Mr. Howe raises a lawn in off hours that reminds one of walking on a Persian rug. They have two sons, Willard and Harold. Both are grown and have homes of their own. Willard lives near his parents but Harold, who is a gifted commercial artist, lives and plies his trade in more commercial lanes.

Mr. Howe has served his patrons long and well, and the time may soon come when he will retire. When he does, we will all be sorry for we know it was a lucky day for the patrons of this route when they hired Mr. Howe. On that day we acquired not just a carrier of the mail, but a friend.

Section II
Anna Scantlin Nolan

Anna Scantlin Nolan

About the middle of the 1800's in the rough and ready days of the logging boom in Northern Michigan, there was a great influx of labor from the more settled parts of the continent. In the midst of those restless times a child was born. This is her story.

Anna Scantlin Nolan was born to Felix Scantlin, a young French Canadian and one of fifteen boys and five girls born to the same parents. Finances had made it necessary for Felix to leave home and support himself when he was quite young, and as many others did, he came down from Canada following the lumber camps. There he built quite a reputation as a first rate "ship timber hewer."

Anna's mother, Mary Traxler, was a native of Pennsylvania Dutch origin who had also been attracted by ready money in the lumber camps and taken employment as a cook's helper.

Employed in the same camp, Felix and Mary were mutually attracted and they soon married and set up housekeeping on a slim budget and a staunch Dunkard belief.

These then, were Anna's parents and this is her background. Anna was the fifth in a family of thirteen born to Felix and Mary Scantlin.

Felix and Mary had migrated as far as Defiance, Ohio when Anna was born in 1880. They couldn't have guessed, as they looked at this new addition to their flock, that she would know more adventure, suffer more trials and see greater triumph over circumstances than they had ever known.

In these days we often hear of the "accident prone" man or woman, but Anna was "prone" to the unusual. Whenever she settled down to an accepted lifestyle, the unexpected took over and new plans were inevitability in order.

Anna was only two years old when her reverse fate began to take a hand, and this event was to leave a mark on her for the rest of her life.

The family lived in a small cabin at the time, which was heated by a fire place and Anna's high chair had been placed near the fireplace and beside a doorway—a heavy traffic area.

As Anna's sister came through the doorway carrying a pan of hot water, Anna's curiosity was aroused. She reached up and grabbed the edge of the pan. "Me see what you got." She pulled at the pan, tipping it so the scalding water poured over her arm, actually cooking the flesh from the wrist to the arm pit.

Her condition was critical and the pain can only be imagined. There was little or no medical aid available at the time, and she could easily have died or lost the use of her arm. But her parents, devout believers, called in their Dunkard minister and he put into practice a method of divine healing known as "Blowing the Fire Out."

This gave Anna relief from the pain and normal healing processes followed. Nevertheless, today there remains a jagged scar and shrunken tissues the length of her left inner arm to prove the seriousness of the burn.

When Anna reached school age, it became increasingly obvious that, although quick to learn, her interests were in action rather than studies and school. School was a place to go only when there was no alternative.

The Scantlin home was near the banks of the Maumee River, and the river became Anna's beloved playground. She became adept at handling a small boat. Plying up and down the river, she investigated the odds and ends that washed ashore, often going aground in the shallows when the river was at flood level.

While still young, a favorite teacher interested Anna in the Catholic belief, and at age 16 she turned from her parents' faith and was confirmed in the Catholic Church. Her confirmation picture shows her to be a very pretty girl but one in which beauty seems second to character.

In 1899, on her 19th birthday, Anna married a neighbor boy named Cassius Bunker and returned to the protestant belief.

For eleven years Anna's life as a wife and mother was sufficient and undisturbed but in 1910 Cassius, urged by a brother who had preceded him, decided to join the western land rush. He acquired property at Bratan, South Dakota and filed his claim. He threw up a sod shanty and sent for Anna and the children.

Anna lost no time packing their furniture which included a new sewing machine, a new set of dishes she had won as a merchant's prize, a good dining room outfit and complete kitchen equipment. These she consigned to a shipping station to be sent by freight while she and the children, with their personal baggage, went by passenger train.

Arriving ahead of their goods, they faced an immediate problem of furnishings which they solved by makeshift means, even eating on large wooden chips with smaller chips for silverware.

For a while it was almost an adventure to get along with these primitive means, but it came as quite a shock when they found that the train carrying their goods had been wrecked at Lemon, South Dakota. Their freight had been completely destroyed by fire.

The loss would have been very serious except for the sympathy and generosity of other homesteaders, who came driving and walking from surrounding claims to present them with all the odd pieces of furniture, dishes and bedding they could spare. With this help Anna and Cassius were able to survive the winter.

The two older children attended school that winter in a fine wooden building. But snow still drifted in around the edges and the ceiling was so low they could reach up and pull straws from between the cracks.

The Bunker homestead was about half a mile from the settlement of Braton. It was bordered on the east by the Cheyenne reservation and on the west by a ranch that was owned by a widow named Smith whose son, Ray, was a Pony Express Rider for the district.

Twice a week Ray brought a bag of mail to Braton. The grocer dumped its contents on the counter and sorted it into the hands of local residents who welcomed the biweekly excuse to gather and talk while they waited for news from the outside.

One mail day Anna, with her baby in her arms and her two older children running alongside, started for the store. As they walked, they watched carefully for rattle snakes, an ever present menace.

The mail was about three hours late and when Ray finally arrived at the store he took special pains to warn Anna not to start home until he was ready to accompany her. A herd of some two hundred wild Cheyenne steers were bunched up in a field between town and her homestead.

Glad for the offer of Ray's company, Anna waited.

When they finally started out, Ray was carrying baby, Thea, on his horse while Anna held Forrest and Faith by their hands.

They hadn't gone far before the steers came into view. As Ray had predicted, they immediately began to show anger at the sight of anyone afoot by bellowing and pawing the dirt. They gradually spread out till they reached a fan formation. Then their heads went down and they charged.

At this point Ray turned and shouted, "Catch!" He threw the baby to Anna and drew his ever present gun. He turned his horse straight into the face of the stampede and galloped forward, shouting and shooting as he went. Anna was sure the next moment would be their last.

Wishing to shield the children from the approaching horror, Anna knelt down and wrapped her arms around them, surrounding them as much as possible with her body.

Minutes passed and dust filled the air until it became nearly unbreathable. Sounds of grunting and churning engulfed them and each moment seemed more certainly their last. Bowing her head, Anna prayed earnestly commending them all to God's mercy.

Finally Anna realized the thunder of hooves had passed them by and she rose unsteadily to her feet. Raising her eyes, she peered across the open prairie to see two separate herds in the diminishing dust clouds. Then she turned to see Ray, unhurt and still on his horse, riding toward her.

Cassius was working hard at the homestead, but it seemed impossible to make ends meet. So one day

Anna took her camera and started out with a horse and buggy. She stopped at each house and offered to take pictures. Later she developed and printed the pictures and sold them. With this additional income, the Bunkers were able to survive the rigors of life on the prairie.

In spite of primitive conditions (the sod shanty, cow chips for fuel etc.) Anna found life on the homestead very interesting. They met such interesting people. Like the time Teddy Roosevelt and his Rough Riders stopped by for a pancake breakfast.

The Bunkers were always finding wonderful and new things like the petrified buffalo head, complete with horns and a lower jaw. Although the family took it with them when they decided to move on, it became such a problem in packing that Anna eventually presented it to Buffalo Bill Cody a year or so before his death.

By this time Anna was expecting her fourth child. She and Cassius were beginning to feel that the homestead was hardly worth the hard labor and the Spartan lack of convenience. And they felt there was little they could do for their children in this undeveloped country. The longer they thought about it, the more they longed for home and the faces and comforts it now represented.

The rules of homesteading demanded a one year residence, five acres of tillable land and a good well. If after filling these requirements you could pay $.50 per acre, it was yours to keep, sell or trade.

Cassius worked from sunup to sundown to finish the required projects. Then they paid up on their land and proceeded at once to mortgage it for $350.00. This money would take care of them for some time. They got their things together and left their homestead with no regrets.

Back in Michigan, the Bunkers soon traded their mortgaged homestead for a house and lot in Adrian. Thus ended the adventure. And they didn't come out too bad either.

Before long Cassius obtained work for the Pillsbury Flour Co. of Detroit. Anna was left alone with the children while Cassius was away on increasingly long selling trips. Frequently he neglected to write or send support for his family, which now included another daughter, Opal.

During one of these times a sympathizing neighbor told Anna of a help wanted ad he had seen in the dining hall at the fair grounds.

When Anna applied for the position as a cook's helper, she was taken on at once and was so efficient that at the end of the week, the owner paid off his chef and took Anna on in his place. As for Anna, she liked the job, she liked the people and she needed the money. So when the fair moved to the next town, Anna went with the rest of the dining crew.

So began a seasonal occupation that helped her through many a tight place, for even after Cassius returned, Anna clung to the job that had been such a life saver.

After three years Anna decided to open her own stand. It displeased the dining hall manager but she never regretted the decision. Times were getting hard and Pillsbury Company, in tightening their expenses laid Cassius off for an indefinite period.

Cassius didn't see much chance of returning to Pillsbury so he got his things together and left once more, ostensibly to look for work in Ohio.

Little did Anna realize, as she bade him good-by, that she would never see him again. Anna was forty years old and expecting another child. She hoped it would be another boy.

As the weeks went by and no money was sent, Anna began to look around for employment. Finally she took two jobs, one in a photographer's studio and the other a night job in the Tuller Hotel.

Anna maintained this demanding schedule for as long as possible. Then, when there seemed no alternative, she took her children and all of her belongings and started north.

Sometime during Anna's marriage her parents, Felix and Mary, had returned to Michigan and taken over forty acres of stump-land near Kalkaska. Near them and directly across from a school was a deserted shack. To the independent Anna this seemed the ideal answer to her needs. Here she unloaded her children and goods. And though the snow sifted in on their beds, she stayed and she kept the older children in school at great expense in money and strength.

When the baby, another girl, was born, Anna went home to her parents. Having girls named Faith and Opal, she named this one Charity. Then as soon as she was able, she went home to her cabin, where she stayed until spring before returning to Detroit to work at the hotel.

When fair season returned she took her children with her and continued her practice of following the fair with her hot dog stand.

But a family of growing children is expensive, and when Anna's income became a mere dribble Anna's married daughter, Thea, urged her to come to Florida.

So Anna took a large sheet of canvas and made a big hamburger and hot dog sign, which she elevated horizontally above her car. Other appliances and supplies were packed so she could set up for business anywhere along the way in twenty minutes flat. Then she started out with her Model T Ford, three children, three dogs and $2.00. As though to warn her of the immensity of her undertaking, she had two flat tires before she even got out of town.

But the biggest problem Anna faced was in keeping a balance between expenses and supplies. She followed behind the fairs as far as Lancaster, Ohio and the end of the fair of the season. There Anna picked up a man named Harmer Judd who insisted they needed his help for the journey. Opal too was quite convinced they could use him.

Now Anna and her family followed a circus and did quite well until they arrived in Washington D.C. There they had to sell one of the dogs, before they could continue their journey.

In South Carolina while traveling in a long line of traffic, the Bunkers came unexpectedly to a toll bridge. Checking their finances, they found they had exactly fourteen dollars—hardly enough to make a dent in the fee. So they offered Anna's beloved camera as security, hoping to stop at the next town, earn a little money and come back to redeem it.

After hearing Anna's story, however, the kindly toll-man let them pass, and that act of kindness made a real difference sometime later when Anna used the camera to obtain rent for a parking space and a supply of groceries.

By this time Anna and her family were getting into the southland where ripe cotton fields covered the countryside and there was plenty of work for transients. So when the next emergency came they stopped for a day and the five of them went to work, hoping to earn enough to take them a good way toward their goal. Imagine their dismay when, after spending the whole day at backbreaking labor, they collected a total of $1.25!!

But they went on their way and only a few days later they pulled into the Tourist Park at Mt. Dora. It was here in this beautiful outdoor setting with the mountains as their background that the romance that had begun in Ohio bloomed. Opal and Harmer spoke their wedding vows.

Anna had expected to return to Michigan after a short visit in Florida, but she found a restaurant job that paid $18.00 a week. It was good wages and beautiful country so she decided to stay until spring. Then she took the remaining children and went back to Michigan.

In 1938, when the fair season was over, the adventuress in Anna again began to beckon. Taking Charity, the only child at home now, she started for California in her Model T. This time she had the misfortune to break her foot after having traveled only as far as Indianapolis, Indiana. She had the foot taken care of and took a bus for the remainder of the trip. They say a good cook can always find a job and she obtained work quickly.

She stayed only until fair time, however, and then she bought another Model T and proceeded to drive it home through dust storms and mountain heights.

The trip to California had satisfied her wanderlust for a time and for the next few years Anna stayed at home in Battle Creek, when not on a fair tour.

Fourteen years after Cassius left, Anna obtained a divorce on grounds of desertion. She had been the sole source of support for her family through good times and bad and now, with only thirteen year old Charity at home, she had more time to think of herself. So, when the circus musician proposed marriage, Anna accepted his proposal, and in 1939 Anna entered into marriage the second time, becoming Mrs. William Nolan.

After this Anna didn't take her stands out with the circus anymore, but continued to run them at the fair. She and William enjoyed twelve years of well adjusted married life. Then in 1941 William collapsed suddenly with a heart attack and Anna was left alone again for by now Charity had married and gone.

In 1947 Anna was thinking strongly again of Northern Michigan. She had always loved Michigan and she bought five acres in Antrim County.

Though the property lay along a roadside, it consisted mostly of second growth trees and a steep hillside, but to Anna it struck a pleasing note. She could picture a home nestled at the foot of the hill and perhaps someday a beautiful building on top with a lift to bring visitors to the door.

So in 1948 at the age of 68 Anna loaded her Model T with tools and cooking utensils and lost no time in getting to her new property. There she parked her car alongside the road and literally "dug in" to the job of building. She slept in the roadside ditch with a shotgun by her side so she might protect her belongings from vandals or marauding animals.

But the building went pretty slowly and the cold weather and fall rains came before Anna could get a roof over her head. She stretched a tarpaulin over three sides of the structure to give her some privacy from the road and some protection from the winds and continued to work.

Then one day the rain was beating down hard and Anna was huddled by her stove with a piece of canvas over her head, when a neighbor, Mr. Jim Mires, stuck his head in the "tent" to see if she was all right.

Miserable but undaunted she replied that she was all right and would yet get her home ready before cold weather.

The picture she left in his mind persisted, however, and the next morning when she started to work, he was there to help. Soon another neighbor came by and stopped to give a hand. One neighbor after another stopped by until there were seven men sawing and fitting and nailing. When evening came, the framework of Anna's house was reflected against the sky.

After that Anna worked with courage and vigor, and sure enough, by snowfall, she had completed the first part of her summer home.

Each year after that, Anna spent several months at her cottage enlarging it and beautifying it. Then one summer she found the limit of her strength. After buying blocks and digging a good sized basement, she suffered a serious heart attack. That convinced her that the basement was not as important as her health. She sold the blocks.

This disappointment was only the beginning, however. Unable to keep going at such a pace, she limited the amount of work and enlarged the cottage no more.

Each summer the local residents looked forward expectantly to the day "Mrs. Nolan" would go rattling by in her jaunty Model T that shone like new and ran like a top. She sat there with her head held high and a ready smile or wave for all she passed.

In May of 1956 Anna was traveling with her brother and his wife when they were involved in a serious accident. She revived in Grand Rapids hospital to find she had a broken arm and two broken legs with one pulverized knee.

Her brother suffered a broken ankle and a chipped hip bone. Her sister in law, who had been thrown through the windshield, had one hundred twenty five stitches in her face.

Five months of hospitalization and many operations followed for Anna. She was unable to run her stand at the fair that year. It was the first year she missed the fair since she started.

But the next year she was back. She had silver plates in her legs and multiple scars but the same courage and the same smile.

In the years since Anna has never failed to visit her northern cottage or to run her stand at the fair. This year on her forty sixth season she was photographed for T.V. by publicity agents from Hagenback and Wallace Circus.

But Anna is afraid this may have been her last year, for the children would like to see her give it up. To many it will come as a sad day and something will be lacking if the fair doesn't include the "good word" and smile, which seem as important as the oyster stew which she served so generously.

Anna has managed with hard work to raise her family well and get a good deal of joy out of life. And although she collected damages from the accident to cover her hospital expenses and a little more, she is not financially well off, which puts her in the "usual" bracket. But in satisfaction and memories, how rich she is! And how few of us will be able to look back on a life as full and rich as hers has been.

Shortly after this was written the author moved to another state and lost track of Anna. I am sure she is gone by now but if anyone is able to finish the story, I would be glad to hear from them.

Section III
The Author's Family

The Author's Parents
Harry & Celestia Batterbee

GRACE

How priceless is the grace of God!
Oh, who can span or weigh?
The riches of His mighty love,
Or who His debt repay?

A love that loved us when the earth
Was void and without form!
Who then devised salvation's plan
To save us from the storm!

A love that sent the Savior down
From Heaven's highest throne
To labor, suffer, watch and pray
And die at last, alone!

A love that spanned the universe,
And fills the realms of space,
And brings to every living soul
The riches of His grace!

Oh how can I such love repay?
I have no price to give,
I can but love Him more and more
And serve Him while I live!

Written by my father
Harry Batterbee

Robert E. Batterbee

As Grandfather Batterbee passed away when my father, Harry Batterbee, was only twelve years old, I have few details of his life. Though I know he traveled to the United States from England.

I remember Daddy telling me his father had been working on a large estate at a construction job. He was pretty young and they had him wheeling heavy loads to the others, when he was noticed and asked if he thought he could lay tile on the roof. He thought he could so they gave him a chance, and he did so well they never let him push a wheelbarrow again.

The only other thing I remember is that he worked in a butcher shop, and that at twenty four years of age he put England behind him, making America his home.

On Grandpa's arrival, he took a job in Chicago in a meat packing plant. Then when the railroads began to hire and to build, he took a job constructing rails into Michigan. Michigan was at that time mainly timber and prairie.

This was hardly a job that could become a life's work and soon Grandpa's wandering eye began to take note of the farm lands that were opening. This was something he knew so he hired out on a farm.

Little did he realize that this decision would affect his whole life, for it was there that he met my grandmother.

One day he was riding down a side road with a team and wagon, when the sky began to grow steadily darker. He looked around to see a group of people looking into the sky, watching an eclipse of the sun.

A young girl who was leaning on a gate caught his eye. He pulled her over the gate and they watched the eclipse together. By the time the eclipse was over, Robert knew this would not be a passing acquaintance.

The young lady was Rosalind Robinson and some months later she and my grandfather were wed.

Grandpa started married life as a bar tender in Three Rivers, Michigan, but after a few months the Baptists held a revival in town. Both he and Grandma attended and gave their lives to the Lord.

One thing from England that Grandfather still held onto was his Methodist heritage, so they joined a Methodist Church and Grandpa was given a "Circuit" of five churches in Northern Michigan.

As horse and buggy were the available means of travel in that undeveloped area, it meant many hours of weary driving for him and many hours of loneliness for Grandma. Distance and poor roads made it advisable to spend the night wherever Grandpa happened to be at nightfall.

Eventually Grandpa dropped off three of the churches. Then with the help of a banker parishioner, he and Grandma settled on a farm near Central Lake. That farm is now known as the Chris Roberts farm.

Grandma ran a small eating place known as Grandma's Table.

Later, as my pa and his siblings grew, Grandpa gave up his churches entirely and the family moved to a farm near East Jordan. As part of the new community, he became a member of the Mackabees, the Masons and the Oddfellows lodges.

But Grandpa caught the flu and he never really recovered. Expenses soon ate up all the resources he and Grandma had saved.

And so it was that at twelve years of age my daddy, Harry Batterbee, became the man of the family.

His brothers, Layland, Earl and Winfred had already married and set up homes of their own. Hazel was in nurses training and Beatrice and Margaret were both still at home. Some years later Grandma remarried but the marriage lasted only a few months.

Daddy never talked about the years after his father died and before he met my mother, but at age twenty two, he met the lady who was to become his life's partner—Celestia Warden, daughter of Willard and Anna Warden. After a two year courtship they were married and in time there were eleven children born to them, of which I was the eldest.

Later Grandmother Warden became ill with TB and she came to our home, where my mother could care for her. I can barely remember Grandma Warden's last days with us.

Willard Warden

In introducing this story I would like to express how pleased I am to be able to give you the story of my own maternal grandparents and great grandparents.

Part of this story I heard many years ago from my great grandmother, the Eunice of this story. The rest of it was told to me by my grandfather, who was the baby, Willard. It may be hard to believe but the puny baby has now lived to the ripe old age of ninety.

As I believe this to be the most complete history I have yet written, I would like to dedicate the story to my mother who is Milo and Eunice's oldest grandchild, and as a mother of eleven, a hero in her own right.

On March 4, 1867, in a cabin located on the east and west borderline between Wisconsin and Minnesota, a baby boy was born to Mr. and Mrs. Milo Warden, a young couple of English New Hampton descent.

The Baby, who was named Willard, had two older siblings, a sister named Emma and a four year old brother named Jasper.

Milo, my great grandfather, was a Civil War veteran who had lately returned from the war. In fact Great Grandfather's return had been without benefit of a discharge. He had become ill while serving in the military and yet had been forced by an autocratic officer to do unnecessary chores. The officer simply wanted to prove his authority.

Knowing that sooner or later Uncle Sam would catch up with him, Great Grandpa Milo was constantly uneasy and becoming more and more eager to move. So when Willard was eight months old, he decided the time had come to leave home and find another place.

Having no team, Great Grandpa Milo turned to the only other possible transportation, a pair of unbroken steers. All the next day, in chilling wind and blowing rain and sleet, Milo fought the animals. Back and forth across the yard he went, with the sleet stinging his face and the cold numbing his fingers. The next morning Milo showed unmistakable signs that he was coming down with a bad cold.

But, miserable or not, Grandpa Milo knew he must waste no time if the move was to be made during that year, so the half broken steers were yoked and loaded; and the long trip was begun.

The storm raged all that day with the wind piling drifts higher and higher in all directions. The cold began to creep into their bones until the blankets and wraps seemed but little protection. As Eunice grew colder, she piled the blankets higher on the children and wrapped Willard a little tighter. Milo stomped his feet to keep them warm.

Finally the light of day faded and the road that had been difficult to track during the daylight hours became nearly impossible to follow in the darkness. The stumbling oxen as well as the children needed food, warmth and rest.

So Grandpa stopped at the next cabin and found a warm welcome.

Eunice and the children were stiff and sore from the long chilling ride. And when Willard was unwrapped, he was unconscious and apparently dead.

Everyone present worked over him desperately for some time. All the while, fear permeated their bones. The children's faces grew white with anxiety.

Finally baby Willard gasped, took a deep breath and returned. The experience left his health seriously impaired for a long time afterward.

Milo's cold was worse now too. The redness of his eyes and his feverish look worried Eunice, but Milo was determined to go on, so the weary worn family climbed into the sleigh the next morning and started on their way. They plodded relentlessly over good roads and bad and finally they reached their destination, Fon-Du-Lac, Wisconsin. They had traveled over one hundred twenty five miles in two days.

Thanksgiving Day that year must have come for them on the day they arrived at Fon-Du-Lac!!

Milo found a place for them to settle and the four walls and a roof must have seemed like heaven.

Eunice tried valiantly to think that everything would be okay, but Milo's cold turned to a hacking cough and tightened down, leaving him barely able to function. Milo tried desperately to stay on his feet to provide fuel and food for his family.

But fate has a way of catching up to us and there came a morning when Milo wasn't able to get out of bed.

The end was not long coming and Eunice, alone now in a strange land, looked down on her sleeping children knowing that it was up to her and her alone to find a way to care for them.

There is one more chapter to be added to the record of Milo Warden, however. For when his death was recorded, Uncle Sam was quick to note and send investigators. After days and weeks of checking on the story Eunice told, it was found that his desertion cast no reflection on the Army itself but was related to only one man. Milo was vindicated and an Honorable Discharge was awarded him posthumously.

Eunice solved her problem of support for her family by taking work with a neighbor, Jabez Bowen and his wife. The work was hard, as she was expected not only to help around the house, but to take the place of their son, who was serving in the army. But she was allowed to take her children with her and that made it worth it all.

In 1869, when Willard was nearly two years old, young George Bowen came home. This was an event that Eunice had feared for some time, wondering where she could find another place to work that would permit her to take her children with her while on the job.

But Mrs. Bowen had grown so used to her help that she was unwilling to let Eunice go, and when George proposed marriage, it seemed the best solution to all their problems.

Trouble hadn't forgotten Eunice and her family, however, for during those years in Fon-Du-Lac, little Emma followed her father in death. This was hard enough for Eunice to bear, but when some childless relatives came visiting, they slipped away in the night taking her son Jasper with them. Eunice was devastated.

Law enforcement officials were unable to apprehend the kidnappers since no one had any idea where they had gone and all indications were that Eunice would never see her child again.

Several years after Jasper disappeared in the night, the Bowens began to receive letters from Michigan. George Bowen's sister, Nancy, as well as some cousins who lived in Lapeer County, wrote enthusiastically about the area, inviting the Bowens to migrate.

Wisconsin had held so much sorrow for Eunice that it held no attraction for her, and George seemed ready to go, as were Jabez and his wife. So it was decided. Both families should make the move to Lapeer County.

There they settled on a farm and Willard still has memories of the great slashings around them. He remembers the Canadian woodsmen, who worked frantically at cutting the big timber and snaking it across the river into Canada on makeshift bridges. They seemed to know that time was short until they would be stopped.

The slash they left behind was a hodgepodge of dead brush and rejected logs and trees—tinder dry—an invitation to disaster.

And the inevitable happened in 1872.

Willard, then five years old, remembers standing in his yard and watching as fire raged for miles up and down the edge of the state. He remembers the fire fighters moving closer and closer.

Eight men worked constantly at different phases of the battle—backfiring, soaking down the house and chasing sparks. The bright flames and the smoke smarted Willard's eyes. The heat was stifling and the roar filled his ears as Willard stood watching with his arm up to shelter his eyes and nose. There was something compelling about the scene. It drew his attention like the flame to a moth.

And then suddenly it was over. The outbuildings were gone; the green fields of crops were gone; only the house behind him was still standing. All around Willard could see nothing but black ashes with little curls of grey smoke rising here and there.

About that time word began to filter through from northern Michigan about a place known as Charlevoix. A veteran can homestead as much as a hundred sixty acres, it was said. Anyone can set up claim stakes on an eighty—wonderful country—good farm land—beautiful—a railroad coming through soon from the south.

All these fragments came together to present a pretty desirable picture to George and Eunice Bowen—and to Charles and Nancy Smith as well who had little left to hold them where they were.

Then one day someone mentioned a man called Pierce who lived in Advance, Michigan. There was no more hesitation for that was the name of the relatives who had taken little Jasper. Jasper would be about ten years old now.

So four families gathered their belongings and headed for Charlevoix County, Jabez Bowen and his wife, George and Eunice Bowen with 5 year old Willard, George's sister, Nancy Smith and her husband, Charles, who had at least two children and Charles' parents.

The trip was one that young Willard never forgot. Made entirely by boat, it consisted of three stages, Saginaw to Mackinaw and Mackinaw to Charlevoix, where they were directed to go down into the bottom of the ship and crawl through a porthole onto the docks. The port was not built to accommodate big boats.

On making inquiry, the group found no overland road to Advance, so they persuaded Johnny Miller who owned a small sail boat to take them to Advance. It wasn't a long trip but when they arrived they found no dock. The only way to get ashore was to wade through water up to their waists, carrying children and luggage. The landing was made on the beach by Johnny Miller's farm, where they stayed while the men built houses.

Finally the Bowens were ready to move, and they asked Joe Sutton to transport their belongings with his team of steers and a two wheeled cart. The site of the Bowen cabin was actually about three and one half miles from Advance, but the only usable road wound around for seven and one half miles.

Willard remembers that trip very well. Though he had sailed over five hundred miles on the Great Lakes, the jolting rocking oxcart was even worse. He became so ill and dizzy he was forced to get off the cart and walk part of the way.

The other buildings in Advance were a grist mill owned by Harry Porter and a store belonging to P.V. Newton.

Later, as more settlers moved in, considerable prejudice developed among the original settlers for the newer ones. Willard remembers one amusing incident of the breakdown of that prejudice. It happened during spearing season.

On the first year that Willard was old enough to be included in the fun, there were still a few of the first settlers. A small group of boys left Willard's house headed for Porter Creek, each one taking practice shots with his spear. On the way they had to pass the house of one of their new neighbors, a young German boy. Halfheartedly they invited him to go along.

Although he had no spear, he agreed.

When they got to the river, the boy didn't hold back but waded right into the current. It was an exciting time as each boy tried to outdo his peers.

Willard felt quite proud of himself for he managed to spear two nice fish.

But the German boy commanded the greatest excitement and admiration of the day. He simply flung his hands into the water, grabbed a fish and held on with might and main. And when he was done he had succeeded in catching one with his bare hands. This feat amazed and delighted the other boys and from then on he was one of the group.

When Willard entered his teens, his health began to improve and he began to show his interest and ability in carpentry and music. It wasn't long before he became known as a first rate "fiddler." He played at all the Grange dances.

When Willard was about twenty, his mother became ill, so he went to Boyne Falls to find someone to help around the house. The girl he brought home was Anna Nowland and before long romance bloomed. On Willard's twenty first birthday they were married.

Willard and Anna found it necessary to follow the wood jobs for a time, including five or six years spent in a wood camp near Hitchcock during its boom years.

In 1901 they returned with their three daughters to the farm, where they stayed until 1917. Willard did some farming and some carpentry, building a number of houses and barns in the area, many of which are still standing.

By then Jasper had married and had a home nearby where he raised three daughters. George and Eunice had moved into East Jordan with their two boys, Ike and Ele, who married and settled in the town.

By then too Willard's older daughters were married. Celestia, the elder, married a lad named Harry Batterbee, son of a Methodist minister. Harry built a home in East Jordan and started their married life as a clerk in a hardware store.

In time, however, he contracted TB and the doctor ordered a move to the country. Harry moved with his family to a farm between East Jordan and Mancelona. And there they lived with their three children.

Lora, the second daughter, lived on a farm with her husband, Roy Hardy, son of a farmer, and their family of two.

By 1917 Willard was having a great deal of trouble with arthritis and there was not much that could be done to help medically. The only advice was a change of climate. After selling their farm and goods, they spent a few weeks visiting their children before starting out for a new home in Virginia. As the oldest grandchild, I remember that visit as though it was yesterday. How I loved to follow Grandpa around.

I remember a day when I heard an unusual noise near our chicken coop, and he helped me follow it up. We searched and searched until finally we looked down into the top of a huge hollow pine stump and right into the beady eyes of a glossy brown mink.

I remember a Sunday, as we were making a buggy trip of about thirty miles to see Aunt Lora and her family, a whipple-tree broke. Grandpa calmly got out of the buggy and made another with his pocket knife. He did it in such a short time that I thought him wonderful.

But all good things must come to an end and in a short time Grandma and Grandpa and their youngest daughter, my aunt Annice, moved to Virginia. They were so far away that I hardly expected to ever see them again. It was twenty eight years before they came back.

Grandpa's health did improve and they spent some of their most enjoyable and productive years in Virginia, as Grandpa pursued his occupation of carpentry.

While they were in Virginia, Great Grandma Eunice suffered a broken hip and finally passed away.

Also, during those years, Annice married a Virginian, Luther Barton. We all debated over and slightly resented him because we had never seen him.

But Annice's troubles soon became equal to her joys. Her little daughter was stricken with infantile paralysis, which left her crippled for life.

Then in 1945 Willard and Anna returned to Michigan and settled in Boyne Falls near Anna's old home.

About a year after the move Annice, who had stayed in Virginia, succumbed to a malignant condition in her throat and Anna followed her daughter in death about a year later after many years of ill health.

Willard stayed on at their home in Boyne. He fished and followed his hobby of woodworking. He made pieces of furniture, cedar chests, bric-a-brac and many fine violins.

Those seven years were full and peaceful years but at eighty six years of age it is not easy to live alone, so when he became ill, Lora and Roy took him to stay with them and he has been with them for three years.

Now ninety years old, he still has that twinkle in his eye and still loves to show off his collection of hand made violins.

Besides his two living daughters, Grandpa has sixteen grandchildren, forty great grandchildren and fifteen great-great grandchildren.

Moving to Camp 18

Thinking perhaps I had better alternate these articles according to length as well as to whether they fall into the pioneer or modern category, I have decided to give you a little bit of personal history. Perhaps it may serve to awaken memories of your own, which need only a twitch to make them alive again.

It goes back to when I was about 6 years old. At that time my father was having a bout with the TB bug. They did not have the knowledge or facilities to care for each case as they do now and it was largely up to the patient to cure himself by means of proper food, fresh air and exercise in big doses.

In my father's case the doctor advised moving to a farm as soon as possible, and that is how I came to find myself riding on a load of furniture into a country such as I had never seen before. You see, father and I had gone on ahead with the wagon-load of furniture, leaving my mother and my two younger brothers to come along later.

In reality it was only a short trip of fifteen miles or so, but on the dirt roads of that time and behind a team of horses which was also a new experience to me, the ride seemed endless. The roads were rough and the load was heavy, so we often stopped to allow the horses to rest.

While it was light, I took turns running along side and riding on the seat beside my father, but when the night came on, I was getting very tired and Daddy made a place for me on the top of the load. I curled up and watched the woods and the stars until I fell asleep. Even after that I half-woke at irregular intervals wondering if we would ever get there. That jolting rumbling ride is one of my clearest memories.

However, I have no recollection of our arrival. I was by that time sound asleep, though I have often wondered how my father got me down off that load without waking me.

The first thing I heard was my father talking to a couple of strange men. As I roused still more, I saw that I was in a strange house lying on a pallet on the floor. For some reason, in my half asleep condition, the strangeness was frightening and I began to cry a little and call my father.

He came at once and assured me that we were with friends. He pointed out that he had covered me with his coat. That coat was all the assurance I needed and, settling down again, I snuggled under the coat feeling as safe as a baby in its mother's arms.

I often think that the journey, as short as it was, must have left me with a similar impression to that of the children of our early settlers. It is one of the favorite memories of my childhood.

Perhaps this memory gave me my intense interest in the people who settled this part of the country.

Couple the memory with the fact that each of the several different farms in the county where I have lived seemed to host the moldering remains of several old homesteads. Add to that the fact that some of those old places were so old that no one seemed to know their origin and you can see a reason for my interest.

Always there was the clearing with at least one gnarled old apple tree and some sign of the means of their water supply. Often I have stood and gazed at the remains of a log cabin or perhaps just a hollow in the ground with a few rotted timbers where the cellar has been, and in my mind they would live again—children scampering in the sun and a mother standing in the doorway shading her eyes with her hand as she tried to see her husband at work in nearby woods or fields. Or perhaps she was watching for him to return from a journey to some far village.

But dreams must give way for reality, and no matter how much we use our imagination in connection with the every day life of those who preceded us in this wonderful part of the country, at least we can say with a surety that they were working with a vision in mind—a vision of rich land converted to easy tillage and a people that were free from bondage and superstition.

With them as our inspiration and God as our help, we should be able to keep both our land and our freedom.

Moving to Camp 18
by Harry Batterbee

Since submitting the material used in this column last week, I have received from my father a more detailed account of the trip to our new home than I, as a child, could possibly have known. After reading it, I wondered if it might not be of more interest than my own account, especially as it throws more light on the adult point of view and emphasizes the difference in the roads and transportation problems of that time—so short a time ago. I think I will let him tell you the story in his own words.

April 19, 1917!! A day we had long looked forward to and a day long to be remembered. We set out early with a heavy load of household goods, including father's library. Grandfather had served as a minister for many years and as such had collected quite a complete ministerial library, which was later inherited by my father.

The weather was cloudy and cold, and our new team was fresh and in high spirits, but eighteen miles is a long way over hills and long stretches of deep sand. The horses were not heavy, just medium weight. John was young and seemed the stronger of the two, but Old Dick was gritty and tough.

Rose, my little six year old daughter, saw many things to interest her naturally inquisitive mind and after our picnic dinner, as the long hours and longer miles stretched out, she found time to make many excursions into the woods and slashings to find the treasures and wonders that are everywhere for a child.

When we came to the part of the country that lies south of Chestonia, the road became very crooked, reminding one of a snake track in the deep sand. The horses were getting very tired by then and John, who had been so fiery in the morning, was beginning to lag. At the beginning of the worst of the way we saw a sign: CHEER UP! THE WORST IS YET TO COME: STROEBEL BROS. That sign remained in place for many years and never failed to bring a smile and memories of our first trip over that road.

By the time we had traversed the sandy part of the road and were facing several miles of hills, John was completely exhausted and discouraged. We stopped to rest every few rods and old Dick would paw and try to go on. Good old Dick! I still remember what a tough old soldier he really was. And he remained the same until the day he died [on his feet] a couple of years later and after several weeks of sickness.

We had been hauling the double buggy behind the wagon all day, and I finally had to hitch the horses to the buggy and leave the wagon by the roadside. By this time it was dark and Rose was asleep, wrapped in a blanket! I guess she never knew when we changed rigs, but she rode the rest of the way propped up on the seat by my side.

John had perked up a bit when we started out with the lighter load and, after a couple of miles, he walked along pretty well. I still think his weariness was mostly discouragement, because he never was a good hauler after that. He'd balk whenever he had an extra hard task.

When we reached the Scott wood-camp, I stopped and hired them to go back and bring my load of goods.

We finally arrived at our new home at about 10:00 PM. Rose was still sleeping; and I carried her into the house and laid her on an improvised pallet on the floor.

We had traveled eighteen miles; it had taken fifteen hours; we had spoiled a good young horse and had to leave our load several miles from its destination. Today the same trip could be made easily in an hour with little cost and much less trouble.

The rest is another story for it was the beginning of a new life for us all and a start on the road back to health for me.

Daddy and Death Hill

This week I have the story of an incident in a camp where my father, Harry Batterbee, worked. It is of the sort which made up the lives of many people during the early years of Antrim County.

There were many men who lost lives and limbs during the removal of the big timber. One woman says, *Many were killed, not because of the great hazards, but unnecessarily because they came into the country knowing nothing whatever about the big timber and ignorant of the safer methods of handling it.* However, finding themselves faced with the problems of removal they refused to back down and did with bull dog persistence a job which might have been less dangerous to men with more knowledge of that type of work. This is a story of a later time when men were growing wise to the problems of lumbering.

Nevertheless, with all their wisdom logging was still a dangerous business and one which called on an individual not only to be prepared to swing every ounce of strength into the balance at the critical time, but also to be able to judge the exact moment that that same strength must be reversed into a backward leap.

My family had lived at Camp eighteen for three years. We had begun clearing stumps and tilling the land but it was winter time and Daddy had gone to work in the lumber camps. The farm was less demanding at that time and the extra income would help bridge the gap until next summer's harvest.

The time is about 1920, when with the greatest share of the big timber already taken off and the market still active, men began to look with hungry eyes at the more difficult locations that had been by-passed the first time over.

The East Jordan Lumber Co. found a good stand on a steep hill which later became known as Death Hill. Found in Echo Township it is not to be confused with Dead Man's Hill, located in the Jordan Valley.

A beautiful stand of hardwood and hemlock, this tract gave promise of being a real paying proposition. That is if it could be logged.

At first glance it seemed so steep as to be impossible. However, the men were determined to at least try! Accordingly, a camp was erected with the buildings about one fourth of a mile north of the work-site. When fully manned and ready for work the camp accommodated about sixty men and probably one to five teams.

The man who bossed the job was Louis Cihak, and of all the others the only names I know are those of my father, Harry Batterbee and his partner Luke DeForest. Luke was a man of about sixty at the time—a jolly fellow and a big favorite with everyone. As amusements were few, it was only to be expected that the men became well acquainted with each other.

The horses also became well known to their handlers, from their first reactions to the harness in the morning to their individual abilities on the steep hillsides or in the boggy valleys. Some were very dependable while others kept a man always on the alert to keep them in control.

As the winter season neared its peak, the swale at the bottom of the steep hill became piled with brush, and the snow on the side hill was traced with logging trails. Many of the great trees on the summit had been laid low.

The steep grade of the hill made the job a dangerous one for horses as well as men, and it had been necessary to install a machine at the top of the hill to let the logs down the hill gradually by means of a steel cable.

It was a bright Monday morning and the horses were feeling high and flighty after a day of rest, but the logging was going on at a good pace just the same. Load after load was lowered from the top of the hill to the bottom, where the cable was unhooked. At this point the team turned left to move the load down the valley toward the decking yard.

The road had been sanded at the top as it was every morning. This was done to provide traction for the loaded sleighs as they were moved into position and the cable attached. It was still quite early in the morning when Old Meanie and Brownie were brought into position with their first load of the day.

Old Meanie was a black that could always make some kind of trouble, although he was capable of a lot of work when kept in control. Because of his experience he had been paired with Brownie, who was new and needed an older horse to keep him in line.

Brownie, who was a beauty, had a disposition that gave great promise of his becoming a really great lumbering horse. This made him the object of everyone's admiration and affection.

When Brownie and Old Meanie came into position, Old Meanie was still smarting from a "tuning up" he had received to quiet his ornery behavior. He was dancing and throwing his head around, keeping the driver busy in an effort to hold him in and at the same time prevent Brownie from getting nervous. So the load passed beyond the sandy spot before the cable operator could hook onto the load.

The sleigh—two eight foot bunks hooked together—was loaded as high as possible with those great logs and the push behind the horses was immense. Though the men tried valiantly to hold steady, and the driver sawed desperately on the lines from his seat high on the load, the 45 degree grade made control a hopeless task.

Finally, when the load was about half way down, the driver recognized the uselessness of it and made a great leap, leaving the load and the horses to their fate.

It was a terrible sight that one could hardly bear to watch. Yet the men could not tear their eyes away. Frozen in their tracks the crew watched, as the load ran up on the horses leaping from hump to hollow like some live thing.

The horses, ran and screamed in fear, but were unable to loose themselves from the monster that followed in relentless pursuit, leaping after them in a fury. It seemed like a nightmare that would never end.

But the end came all too soon. As the horses reached the bottom of the hill, they could not make the turn. They hit the bend with full force and took one final leap high into the air, hurtling over a great brush heap and landing in a tangle of brush, logs, sleighs and horses.

For a moment the quiet was like a shock to the ears of the men, who were standing like figures in a wax museum. The only conscious thought was a hopeless wish to see Brownie emerge unhurt.

Several minutes passed before any movement was seen. Then from the tangle a horse was seen getting to its feet. In a moment more they could see that the survivor was the veteran, Old Meanie. The men looked in vain for any movement from the heap that used to be Brownie.

Old Meanie stood slowly to his feet, stood a moment with his head hung low, as though he too mourned. Then he shook himself free of his harness and started on a trot to the barn.

The incident was over, and another load now pulled into position for the double hook. The driver was safe and even though one horse was lost, Old Meanie would take many more loads down the hill.

And the work would go on. The impossible hill, had met its irrevocable fate.

A TRUE FRIEND

I have found a Friend.
Not just a "friendly friend," but a Friend!
Somehow, He's given me a new light
On what true "friendship" means.
        It has changed me!

True friendship helps us grow,
It enriches life and widens the scope of our interest,
But most of all it helps us know
That whatever life holds for you;
You can bear it, because,
        You have a Friend!

Other Titles by
Dawn Batterbee-Miller

God's Family Tree – Out of Print

Footprints Under The Pines

A publication of WinePress Group

<u>Coming Soon</u>

The Sequal to Footprints Under The Pines

<u>Contact:</u>

http://www.DawnCreations.net

.